Best Easy Day Hikes Series

Best Easy Day Hikes
Acadia National Park

Second Edition

Dolores Kong
Dan Ring

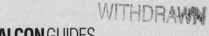

FALCONGUIDES

GUILFORD, CONNECTICUT
HELENA, MONTANA
AN IMPRINT OF GLOBE PEQUOT PRESS

FALCONGUIDES®

Copyright © 2001, 2011 by Morris Book Publishing, LLC

FalconGuides is an imprint of Globe Pequot Press.
Falcon, FalconGuides, and Outfit Your Mind are registered trademarks
of Morris Book Publishing, LLC.

Maps by Design Maps Inc. © Morris Book Publishing LLC
Project editor: Julie Marsh
Layout artist: Kevin Mak

Library of Congress Cataloging-in-Publication Data
Kong, Dolores.
  Best easy day hikes, Acadia National Park / Dolores Kong, Dan Ring.
      p. cm. — (FalconGuides)
  ISBN 978-0-7627-6132-6
  1. Hiking—Maine—Acadia National Park—Guidebooks. 2. Trails—
Maine—Acadia National Park—Guidebooks. 3. Acadia National Park
(Me.)—Guidebooks. I. Ring, Dan (Daniel) II. Title.
  GV199.42.M22A323 2011
  796.5109741'45—dc22

                                              2010042878

Printed in the United States of America

10 9 8 7

Contents

Help Us Keep This Guide Up to Date

Every effort has been made by the authors and editors to make this guide as accurate and useful as possible. However, many things can change after a guide is published—trails are rerouted, regulations change, facilities come under new management, etc.

We would appreciate hearing from you concerning your experiences with this guide and how you feel it could be improved and kept up to date. While we may not be able to respond to all comments and suggestions, we'll take them to heart and we'll also make certain to share them with the authors. Please send your comments and suggestions to the following address:

> GPP
> Reader Response/Editorial Department
> P.O. Box 480
> Guilford, CT 06437

Or you may e-mail us at:
> editorial@GlobePequot.com

Thanks for your input, and happy trails!

Acknowledgments

For sharing with us their knowledge and passion for Acadia National Park, and being so generous with their time, we'd like to thank Wanda Moran, Charlie Jacobi, Gary Stellpflug, Kathy Grant, Stuart West, Karen Anderson, Anne Warner, and the rest of the Acadia National Park staff; Margaret Coffin Brown of the Olmsted Center for Landscape Preservation; Ann Marie Cummings of Eastern National; and Marla S. O'Byrne of the Friends of Acadia.

And we'd like to thank our nieces Sharon and Michelle Kong. We hope they've come away with some special memories of Acadia.

Introduction

Maine's Acadia National Park is a place like no other.

You can stroll along Ocean Path and be awestruck by the contrast of pink granite cliffs, blue skies, and white surf. From atop Cadillac, the highest mountain on the Atlantic seaboard, you can see fog rolling in over Frenchman Bay below, even as the sun shines brightly above. And over on the shores of Jordan Pond, you can take part in one of the most civilized of afternoon rituals, tea and popovers, with the distinct mountains known as the Bubbles as nature's backdrop.

No wonder artists, millionaires, generations of families, and even presidents have been attracted to all that's preserved in Acadia.

In fact, the place has meant so much to area residents and visitors that Acadia became the first national park created east of the Mississippi, in 1919. It is also the first national park to consist primarily of privately donated lands, and the first to have trail maintenance funded by an endowment, Acadia Trails Forever, coming from $4 million in park user fees and federal appropriations and $9 million in private donations from Friends of Acadia, a private nonprofit organization based in Bar Harbor.

Over the years the scenery here has inspired such passion that nineteenth-century painters Thomas Cole and Frederic Church, of the Hudson River School, came here to capture the landscape; one of the wealthiest men in America, John D. Rockefeller Jr., donated millions and left miles of picturesque carriage roads and uniquely designed stone bridges; and George B. Dorr, prime mover behind creating the national park, spent his inheritance on the park and wouldn't have been able to pay for his own funeral if his estate's trustee hadn't set aside $2,000 for that purpose, as highlighted in the PBS documentary *The National Parks: America's Best Idea,* by Ken Burns and Dayton Duncan.

The scenery at Acadia even drew President Barack Obama and his family in July 2010 to the views from the top of Cadillac and along the Ship Harbor and Bass Harbor Head Light Trails.

As part of the Centennial Initiative to mark the hundredth anniversary of the National Park Service in 2016, Acadia plans to preserve and pass on the passion in a number of ways: acquiring more land, establishing more village connector trails and otherwise encouraging car-free use, and creating programs to foster young conservationists and scientists. The year 2016 also marks the hundredth anniversary for Acadia, since it was first founded as the Sieur de Monts National Monument in 1916.

Today about two million visitors a year make Acadia one of the top-ten most visited national parks, even though it's the fifth smallest in land area, according to "A Guide's Guide to Acadia National Park," available online at www .nps.gov/acad. But with more than 125 miles of hiking trails and 45 miles of carriage roads throughout its approximately 49,500 acres (including about 12,000 acres under conservation easement), the park provides plenty of opportunities for tranquility and experiencing the many aspects of nature, history, geology, and culture.

This guide is for those with limited time to hike Acadia, or for those who want to sample only the easiest or most popular trails. This second edition of *Best Easy Day Hikes Acadia National Park* was researched as part of an update of our more comprehensive guide, *Hiking Acadia National Park*. While the bigger book covers nearly all of the park's trails, including those in the harder-to-reach parts of the park like Isle au Haut, this guide includes just the best easy or most popular hikes in the main part of Acadia, on Mount Desert Island. Also excluded from this guide are the strenuous cliff climbs that are in *Hiking Acadia National Park* and the 45 miles of carriage roads that are also used by bicyclists, horseback riders, and horse-drawn carriages.

Many of the trails described here are very easy and suitable for families with young children, but some are more challenging hikes that are among the most popular in the area, bringing you to grand mountaintop vistas. The "Trail Finder" section of this guide offers a listing of hikes by characteristic, such as "Best Hikes for Children" or "Best Hikes for Great Views."

Since the first edition of this guide, new trails have been added and trail names have been changed to reflect a comprehensive multiyear, multimillion-dollar effort by the National Park Service and Acadia Trails Forever to update the historic network. The extensive system includes Native American paths, old roads, and trails built by local village improvement associations near the turn of the twentieth century, as documented by the National Park Service's Olmsted Center for Landscape Preservation.

For example, Schooner Head Path is a recently reopened trail that dates back to 1901, a section of which is included in this guide for the first time. And what was called the Bear Brook Trail in the first edition is now the Champlain North Ridge Trail, as already reflected on trailhead signs.

But a note of caution: In some cases the Park Service may not yet have updated trail signs—it's a multiyear process—even though the plan is to ultimately rename some of the historic trails. For that reason the old trail names are listed in this guide in parentheses for reference.

We've also added to this edition the Compass Harbor Trail, which takes visitors by the remains of Old Farm, the family residence of George B. Dorr, the "father of Acadia National Park"; and the recently opened Great Meadow Loop, which incorporates a historic section of Jesup Path.

Another addition: mention of Island Explorer bus stops near trailheads, if you visit during peak season and want to take advantage of this increasingly popular, free, and eco-friendly way of getting around Acadia. The bus driver may also make specially requested stops, if it's safe to do so. Be sure to buy a park pass to help support the Island Explorer and other programs offered by the Park Service.

Aside from hiking some of the trails described here, visitors may also want to stop at the Abbe Museum, the Wild Gardens of Acadia, and the Nature Center, all located at the Sieur de Monts entrance to the park, on ME 3 south of Bar Harbor.

The Abbe Museum, founded by Dr. Robert Abbe, a pioneer of the medical use of radium, celebrates and preserves the culture and heritage of Native Americans who lived here thousands of years before European settlers set eyes on the Maine coast. In addition to the seasonal museum at the Sieur de Monts Spring entrance, there is a year-round museum facility in downtown Bar Harbor.

The Wild Gardens of Acadia and the Nature Center introduce the visitor to some of the flora and fauna of Acadia. The whole Sieur de Monts Spring area, especially the gardens in early morning, is an excellent bird-watching spot, with the possibility of sighting warblers, woodpeckers, flycatchers, and thrushes.

Weather

In the space of an hour or less, the weather in Acadia can change from sunny and warm to wind-whipped rain, especially on mountaintops. Summer highs average seventy to eighty degrees Fahrenheit, although fog can be common, with lows in the fifties. In the spring, highs average fifty to sixty degrees Fahrenheit, and it can be rainy. The fall brings highs in the low seventies, but rain or snow can be expected. In the winter, temperatures range from below zero to thirty degrees Fahrenheit, and snowfall averages about 60 inches a year.

Rules and Regulations

Pets must be kept on a leash no longer than 6 feet and are not allowed on ladder trails or in public water supplies. They are also prohibited from Sand Beach and Echo Lake from May 15 to September 15; public buildings; ranger-led programs; and the Wild Gardens of Acadia. (Service animals are an exception to these rules.) The Park Service is continually reevaluating the pet policy. Be sure to follow the rules, or you can ruin the visit for other hikers and pet owners or harm your pet and wildlife.

Parking, camping, and fires are only allowed in designated spots. No camping is allowed in the backcountry, only in Seawall Campground (closed in winter) and Blackwoods Campground (open year-round but with primitive camping only from December 1 through March 31).

Firearms are prohibited in the park, unless they are packed away, broken down, or otherwise unable to be used, or unless other exceptions under federal and Maine law apply.

Safety and Preparation

Use caution near cliffs and water's edge, especially during stormy weather. People have been swept to sea by storm-driven waves. Don't turn your back on the ocean.

Wear proper footwear, ideally hiking boots, especially for the more challenging hikes, but sneakers or some other sturdy closed-toe, rubber-soled shoe may be suitable for the easiest hikes. Trails and rocks can be slippery, especially when wet. Loose gravel on rocks can also be dangerous. Most injuries come from falls while hiking or biking.

Carry at least one quart of water per person. Do not count on finding water on any hike, but if you must use natural water sources, treat with water purifiers or iodine tablets before consumption.

Wear sunscreen and protective clothing, especially a hat, to protect against the potentially harmful effects of overexposure to the sun.

Dress in layers and pack rain gear so that you are prepared for changes in weather. Bring extra socks and clothing.

If you hike alone, tell a reliable person your hiking plans, especially if you will be hiking in the more remote areas. Stick to your plan when you are on the hike, and be sure to check in upon your return.

Do not leave valuables in your car.

Day Hiker Checklist

- ❏ Daypack
- ❏ Food
- ❏ First-aid kit
- ❏ Insect repellent
- ❏ Headlamp or flashlight
- ❏ Camera
- ❏ Binoculars
- ❏ Trail guide
- ❏ Detailed trail map
- ❏ Compass or GPS unit
- ❏ Signal mirror
- ❏ Toilet paper and zippered plastic bags
- ❏ Sun hat
- ❏ Cell phone for emergencies

Leave No Trace

Many of the trails in Acadia National Park are heavily used, particularly in the peak summer months into September. We, as trail users and advocates, must be especially vigilant to make sure our passage leaves no lasting mark.

Follow these Leave No Trace principles:

- Leave with everything you brought.
- Leave no sign of your visit.
- Leave the landscape as you found it.

And here are some additional guidelines for preserving trails in the park:

- Pack out all your own trash, including biodegradable items like orange peels. You might also pack out garbage left by less-considerate hikers.

- Don't approach or feed any wild creatures—the ground squirrel eyeing your snack food is best able to survive if it remains self-reliant. Plus it's prohibited in the park.

- Don't pick wildflowers or gather rocks, shells, and other natural or historic features along the trail. Removing these items will only take away from the next hiker's experience. Plus it's prohibited in the park.

- Don't alter the cairns, or piles of rocks that serve as trail markers, or create new ones.

- Avoid damaging trailside soils and plants by remaining on the established route.

- Walk single file in the center of the trail.

- Don't cut switchbacks, which can promote erosion.

- Be courteous by not making loud noises or casual cell phone calls while hiking.

- Many of these trails are shared with trail runners and dog walkers, and some are accessible to visitors with wheelchairs or baby strollers.

- Familiarize yourself with the proper trail etiquette, yielding the trail when appropriate.

- Use facilities at trailheads where available. Bury human waste in areas without toilets, and pack out toilet paper.

- Pick up after pets.

Visitor Information

Information about the park may be obtained by contacting Acadia National Park, P.O. Box 177, Bar Harbor, ME

04609-0177. The telephone number is (207) 288-3338, and the website is www.nps.gov/acad.

The Hulls Cove Visitor Center is located on ME 3, northwest of Bar Harbor. It is open from 8:00 a.m. to 4:30 p.m. daily from mid-April through June and in October. It is open from 8:00 a.m. to 6:00 p.m. daily in July and August and 8:00 a.m. to 5:00 p.m. daily in September.

The Winter Visitor Center is at Acadia National Park headquarters on ME 233, west of Bar Harbor. It is open from 8:00 a.m. to 4:30 p.m. daily from November through mid-April and is closed Thanksgiving Day, December 24 and 25, and January 1. It is also open from 8:00 a.m. to 4:30 p.m. Monday through Friday from mid-April through October.

Some hiking trails and parts of the 27-mile Park Loop Road are seasonally closed or may be closed for safety reasons or to protect nesting peregrine falcons. Check for trail and road closures with National Park Service officials or at www.nps.gov/acad.

Park entrance fees apply between May 1 and October 31, with a seven-day pass available for one vehicle; a seven-day pass for one individual on foot, motorcycle, or bicycle; and an annual pass for one vehicle.

From late June to early October, the free Island Explorer bus operates between points on Mount Desert Island and the park. For schedules, routes, stops, and other information, go to www.exploreacadia.com.

Hikers also might find the detailed United States Geological Survey map of the park helpful. The park's visitor center sells the USGS Acadia National Park and Vicinity map, along with other maps and literature.

How to Use This Guide

This guide is designed to be simple and easy to use.

Each hike is described with a map and summary information that delivers the trail's vital statistics including length, difficulty, and canine compatibility.

Directions to the trailhead are also provided, along with a general description of what you'll see along the way. A detailed route finder ("Miles and Directions") sets forth mileage between significant landmarks along the trail.

Trailhead GPS coordinates listed in the "Finding the trailhead" section of each hike description are based on data collected by us, provided by Acadia National Park, or gathered from other reliable sources, such as the website of the U.S. Board of Geographic Names, http://geonames .usgs.gov/.

But as with any GPS data provided for recreational use, there are no warranties, expressed or implied, about data accuracy, completeness, reliability, or suitability. The data should *not* be used for primary navigation. Readers of this guide assume the entire risk as to the quality and use of the data.

Acadia National Park officials advise that visitors obey posted signs and park regulations, pay attention to common sense, and avoid accidentally traveling on private lands while using a GPS unit.

Difficulty Ratings

These are all easy hikes, but easy is a relative term. To aid in the selection of a hike that suits particular needs and abilities, each is rated easy, moderate, or more challenging. Bear in mind that even the most challenging routes can be made easy by hiking within your limits and taking rests when you need them.

Easy hikes are generally short and flat, taking no longer than one to two hours to complete.

Moderate hikes involve relatively mild changes in elevation and will take one to two and a half hours to complete.

More challenging hikes feature some steep stretches, greater distances, and generally take longer than two and a half hours to complete.

These are completely subjective ratings—consider that what you think is easy is entirely dependent on your level of fitness and the adequacy of your gear (primarily shoes). If you are hiking with a group, you should select a hike with a rating that's appropriate for the least fit and prepared in your party.

Approximate hiking times are based on the assumption that on flat ground, most walkers average 2 miles per hour. Adjust that rate by the steepness of the terrain and your level of fitness (subtract time if you're an aerobic animal and add time if you're hiking with kids), and you have a ballpark hiking duration. Be sure to add more time if you plan to picnic or take part in other activities like bird watching or photography.

Trail Finder

Best Hikes for Great Views

Best Hikes for Children

Best Hikes for Dogs

Best Hikes for History and Geology Buffs

2   Jesup Path to Great Meadow Loop

3   Compass Harbor Trail

4   Cadillac Summit Loop Trail

11   Gorham Mountain Trail

Best Hikes for Peak Baggers

4   Cadillac Summit Loop Trail

6   Champlain North Ridge Trail

11   Gorham Mountain Trail

14   Bubbles Divide

15   Acadia Mountain Trail

16   Flying Mountain Trail

18   Beech Mountain Loop Trail

Best Hikes for Lake and Ocean Lovers

1   Bar Island Trail

8   Sand Beach and Great Head Trail

9   Ocean Path

10   The Bowl Trail

13   Jordan Pond Path

19   Wonderland

20   Ship Harbor Trail

Best Hikes for Nature Lovers

2   Jesup Path to Great Meadow Loop

12   Jordan Pond Nature Trail

Map Legend

━━━③━━━	State Highway
━━━━━━	Local Road
= = = = = :	Unpaved Road
▬▬▬▬▬	Featured Trail
- - - - - - -	Trail
~~	River/Creek
─ · ─ · ─	Intermittent Stream
▲ ⌐	Marsh
▭▭▭	National Park
⇶	Boat Ramp
▲	Campground
⛦	Lighthouse
▲	Mountain/Peak
🅿	Parking
⌁	Picnic Area
■	Point of Interest/Structure
🕼	Restaurant
🚻	Restroom
⚬⌐	Spring
○	Town
⓫	Trailhead
🮻	Tower
☎	Telephone
⚘	Viewpoint
❓	Visitor/Information Center
⋙	Waterfall

Mount Desert Island East of Somes Sound

Most of Acadia National Park's trails, the main Park Loop Road, and many of the best views are here on the eastern half of Mount Desert Island. Most of the "best easy" hikes are also located here.

The various hikes in this section are grouped into three geographic divisions: the Bar Harbor / Cadillac and Champlain Mountains area; the Gorham Mountain area; and the Jordan Pond and Bubbles area.

From trails in the Bar Harbor / Cadillac and Champlain Mountains area, you can get some of Acadia's best-known views of Bar Harbor, Frenchman Bay, and the Porcupine Islands. The park's Sieur de Monts entrance is also here, allowing access to the Wild Gardens of Acadia, the Nature Center, and the Abbe Museum.

The Gorham Mountain area features such seashore hikes as Sand Beach and Great Head Trail and the very easy Ocean Path, as well as such moderate hikes as the Gorham Mountain Trail.

At the heart of the Jordan Pond and Bubbles area is the Jordan Pond House, famous for its afternoon tea and pop-overs and its view of the twin peaks known as the Bubbles. The Jordan Pond House serves as a jumping-off point for a couple of easy trails. Other dominant features accessible by trails in this area include a precariously perched rock known as Bubble Rock.

1 Bar Island Trail

A low-tide walk leads to a rocky island off Bar Harbor, providing a unique perspective back toward town and its mountain backdrop. The trail can also offer a close-up view of seagulls feeding, as they drop mussels from midair to crack open the shells.

Distance: 2.0 miles out and back
Approximate hiking time: 1 to 1.5 hours
Difficulty: Easy
Trail surface: Low-tide gravel bar, gravel road, forest floor, rock ledges
Best season: Spring through fall
Other trail users: Joggers, motorists on gravel bar, owners of private homes on Bar Island
Canine compatibility: Leashed dogs permitted

Map: USGS Acadia National Park and Vicinity
Special considerations: Accessible only 1.5 hours on either side of low tide. Check tide chart on Bar Island; in the seasonal park newspaper, *The Beaver Log;* or at http://maineboats.usharbors.com/monthly-tides/Maine-Downeast. There is a public restroom at the intersection of West and Main Streets.

Finding the trailhead: From ME 3 at the park visitor center, head south for about 2.5 miles, toward downtown Bar Harbor. Turn left (east) onto West Street, which is at the first intersection after the College of the Atlantic. The trail, visible only at low tide, leaves from Bridge Street, the first left off West Street on the edge of downtown. There is limited on-street parking on West Street. The closest Island Explorer stop is Bar Harbor Village Green, which is available on the Campgrounds, Eden Street, Sand Beach, Jordan Pond, Brown Mountain, and Southwest Harbor lines. **GPS:** N44 39.18' / W068 20.98'

The Hike

The Bar Island Trail is a short easy jaunt within shouting distance of Bar Harbor, but you feel transported to another world. That is the beauty of being on an island, even a small one so close to a busy summer resort town.

Easy enough for the least-seasoned hiker, the Bar Island Trail also provides a bit of risk to satisfy the thrill-seeking adventurer—it can only be traveled at low tide, when a gravel bar connecting Bar Harbor and the island is exposed. CAUTION! a sign warns hikers once they reach the island's rocky shores. SAFE CROSSING IS 1.5 HOURS ON EITHER SIDE OF LOW TIDE. CHECK TIDE CHART FOR DAILY TIDE TIME! CAUTION! For your convenience, a tide chart is posted.

Another bit of risk to caution you about, as our nieces Michelle and Sharon experienced while walking along the gravel bar: Watch out for seagulls feeding nearby—or you may find a mussel being dropped on your shoulder.

First described in 1867, the trail was reopened by the National Park Service in the 1990s.

From the foot of Bridge Street in Bar Harbor, walk northwest across the gravel bar, reaching the island at about 0.4 mile. Some of the resort town's historic summer "cottages"— really mansions—are visible along Bar Harbor's shoreline to the left (southwest) as you cross the gravel bar.

Once you reach Bar Island, head northeast up the gravel road behind the gate. The trail soon levels off at a grassy field. At about 0.6 mile, bear left (northeast) at a trail sign pointing into the woods toward Bar Island summit. At a fork at about 0.8 mile, marked by a cairn (or pile of rocks to mark a change in trail direction), bear right (southeast) up a rocky knob.

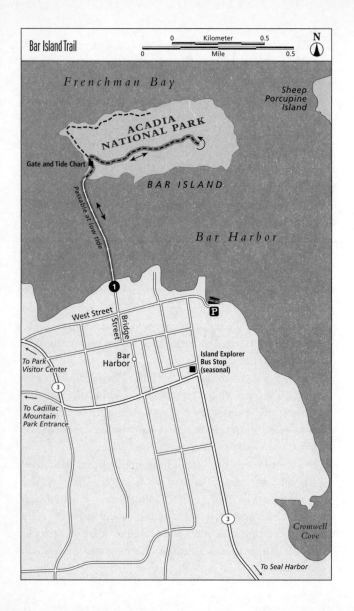

At about 1.0 mile, you reach the summit, with its views toward Bar Harbor. From here you can hear the town's church bells, see the fishing and recreational boats along the harbor, and take in the smells of the sea and the views of the mountains.

Return the way you came.

Miles and Directions

0.0   Bar Island trailhead, at the foot of Bridge Street.

0.4   Reach the shore of Bar Island. Check the posted tide chart to time your return, else you'll have to wait more than twelve hours for the next low tide. Head northeast up the gravel road behind the gate.

0.6   Cross a grassy field and come to a junction; bear left (northeast) into the woods at the trail sign.

0.8   Reach another junction marked by a cairn; bear right (southeast) up to the island's summit.

1.0   Reach the island's summit, with views back toward Bar Harbor and the mountains.

2.0   Return to the trailhead.

2 Jesup Path to Great Meadow Loop

This woods, wetlands, and field walk takes you by Sieur de Monts Spring, the Wild Gardens of Acadia, the Nature Center, and the Abbe Museum and along the recently opened Great Meadow Loop. You'll hear birdsong and get open views of Huguenot Head and Champlain and Dorr Mountains along Great Meadow. And you can re-create the historic experience of walking between Bar Harbor and the park, like the residents and visitors of yore.

Distance: 3.1-mile lollipop
Approximate hiking time: 1.5 to 2 hours
Difficulty: Easy
Trail surface: Forest floor, graded gravel path, wooden boardwalk and bridges
Best season: Spring through fall, particularly early morning or late afternoon in the summer to avoid the crowds
Other trail users: Dog walkers, joggers, area residents

Canine compatibility: Leashed dogs permitted (but not in the Wild Gardens of Acadia, Nature Center, or Abbe Museum)
Map: USGS Acadia National Park and Vicinity
Special considerations: Graded gravel and wooden boardwalk surfaces make part of the walk wheelchair and baby-stroller accessible. Seasonal restrooms are at the Sieur de Monts parking area.

Finding the trailhead: From downtown Bar Harbor head south on ME 3 for about 2 miles and turn right (west) into the park's Sieur de Monts entrance. From the parking area walk behind the Nature Center and follow the wooden sign pointing right (west) toward trails, over a small wooden bridge and past a stone inscribed with the words SWEET WATERS OF ACADIA AND THE SIEUR DE MONTS SPRING HOUSE. Follow the Emery Path for a short distance to the base of the stone steps that go up Dorr Mountain, and turn right (north) onto Jesup

Path. The Island Explorer's Sand Beach and Loop Road lines stop at Sieur de Monts. **GPS:** N44 36.20' / W068 20.81'

The Hike

First created nearly one hundred years ago by George B. Dorr and others as part of a garden path that connected to downtown Bar Harbor, Jesup Path runs between the Tarn and the Park Loop Road and links to the Great Meadow Loop.

The hike described here picks up the Jesup Path at the easy-to-reach Sieur de Monts parking area, just shy of its southern terminus at the Tarn, and takes you 0.7 mile north to the one-way Park Loop Road and around the 1.7-mile Great Meadow Loop.

The loop, partly on park land and partly on private property, recently opened through the efforts of the Friends of Acadia and park officials. It helps reconnect the park to the outskirts of Bar Harbor, as had been the case historically.

From the Jesup Path trailhead at Sieur de Monts, at the base of the stone steps up Dorr Mountain, head north (right) along the western edge of the Wild Gardens of Acadia. Then cross a junction with the gravel Hemlock Road and follow a long wooden boardwalk through a wooded wetland. The trail then crosses Hemlock Road again and becomes gravel-based.

You'll find plenty of birds and flowering plants along the marshy "meadow," especially in spring. And as you approach the northern terminus of Jesup Path by the one-way Park Loop Road, look back over the Great Meadow toward the Sieur de Monts area and you'll find open views of Huguenot Head and Champlain Mountain to the east (left) and Dorr Mountain to the west (right).

Cross the one-way Park Loop Road and turn left to go clockwise around the 1.7-mile Great Meadow Loop. The loop takes you through deciduous forest, by the Kebo Valley Golf Club; two cemeteries, near Kebo and Cromwell Brooks; and along and across less-traveled paved roads on the outskirts of Bar Harbor.

The Great Meadow Loop is just one of the village connector trails being re-created as part of the $13 million Acadia Trails Forever initiative, a joint effort of the Friends of Acadia and the National Park Service. The idea: to give residents and visitors options for walking between town and the mountains, ponds, and sea, as was the case during the days of the nineteenth- and early-twentieth-century rusticators, or artists, tourists, and summer residents, who would think nothing of walking 5, 10, or 15 miles in a day.

Once you circle back on the Great Meadow Loop to the junction with the Jesup Path, cross back over the one-way Park Loop Road and head south on the path.

Return to the Sieur de Monts Spring area, for a 3.1-mile round-trip.

Miles and Directions

0.0 Jesup Path trailhead is at a junction with Emery Path, at the base of the stone steps up Dorr Mountain. Head north (right) and follow the western edge of the Wild Gardens of Acadia.

0.1 Cross over a junction with the gravel Hemlock Road and walk along the long wooden boardwalk.

0.5 Reach the end of the boardwalk, cross another junction with Hemlock Road, and continue straight (north) on a graded gravel path toward the Park Loop Road.

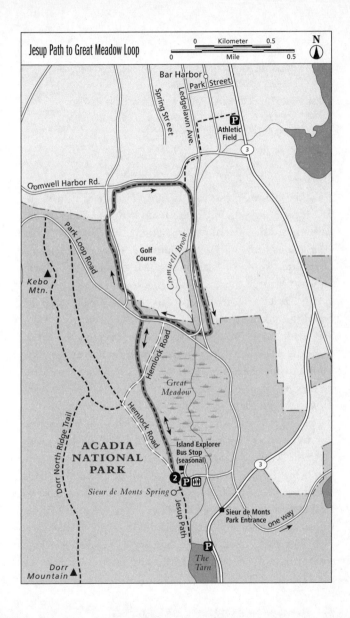

Jesup Path to Great Meadow Loop

0   Kilometer   0.5
0   Mile   0.5

N

Bar Harbor
Park Street

Spring Street

Ledgelawn Ave.

P
Athletic
Field

3

Cromwell Harbor Rd.

Park Loop Road

Golf
Course

Cromwell Brook

Kebo
Mtn.

Hemlock Road

Great
Meadow

Hemlock Road

Dorr North Ridge Trail

ACADIA
NATIONAL
PARK

Island Explorer
Bus Stop
(seasonal)

2 P

Sieur de Monts Spring

Sieur de Monts
Park Entrance   one way

3

Jesup Path

P

Dorr
Mountain

The Tarn

0.7 Cross the Park Loop Road to connect with the 1.7-mile Great Meadow Loop, and turn left to go around the loop clockwise as it goes along park and private property and crosses less-used paved roads.

2.4 Circle back to Jesup Path's junction with the Park Loop Road, and cross the one-way road to head south back toward Sieur de Monts Spring.

3.1 Return to the trailhead.

Options

To add a 0.3-mile spur to the Tarn, head south from Sieur de Monts Spring on either the Jesup Path or Wild Gardens Path toward that glacially carved pond in the gorge between Huguenot Head and Dorr Mountain. A plaque at this end of the trail reads In Memory of Morris K. and Maria DeWitt Jesup, Lovers of this Island, 1918.

Or create a shorter loop than the one described here. From the northern terminus of Jesup Path, cross the one-way Park Loop Road and turn right (east) on the Great Meadow Loop for 0.1 mile, then cross back over the Park Loop Road to take the gravel Hemlock Road back to Sieur de Monts.

Or do the same 3.1-mile hike but in reverse, as if a modern-day rusticator walking from town to mountains, ponds, or sea. You can park at the ball fields on ME 3 south of town. Walk west on Park Street, south on Ledgelawn, and west on Cromwell Harbor Road to reach the Great Meadow Loop trailhead just before (east of) Ledgelawn Cemetery in about 0.4 mile. Some of the 0.4 mile is along sidewalks, and some along the side of the road, so take care, especially along Cromwell Harbor Road. You can get more information about the Great Meadow Loop by contacting the Friends of Acadia at (207) 288-3340.

3 Compass Harbor Trail

Situated just outside Bar Harbor, this easy trail offers both important history—it's the former site of park pioneer George B. Dorr's estate—and sweeping ocean views—its point is right on Frenchman Bay. The trail features some remnants of Dorr's family home, older growth trees, Dorr Point, and sights along the bay. The Compass Harbor Trail is usually among the less-frequented areas of the park.

Distance: 0.8 mile out and back
Approximate hiking time: 30 minutes
Difficulty: Easy
Trail surface: Gravel road, forest floor, sandy trail at end
Best season: Spring through fall, particularly off-peak times

Other trail users: Dog walkers, joggers, area residents
Canine compatibility: Leashed dogs permitted
Map: USGS Acadia National Park and Vicinity
Special considerations: No facilities

Finding the trailhead: From downtown Bar Harbor head south on ME 3 for 1.0 mile. A parking lot is located on the left (east) just after Nannau Wood, a private road, and just before Old Farm Road, also private. The trail begins off the parking lot. If the parking lot is full, you can park at the town ball fields and walk south just over 0.5 mile along ME 3 to the trailhead. The Island Explorer bus does not have a stop here, although the Sand Beach line goes by and you may be able to ask the bus driver to let you off if it is safe to do so. **GPS:** N44 37.38' / W068 19.76'

The Hike

Standing out over Compass Harbor, you can imagine park trailblazer George B. Dorr taking his daily swim in the cold waters of Frenchman Bay or tending to the gardens that once surrounded his home here.

The trail begins as a wide gravel road off the parking lot and soon comes to a sign pointing to Compass Harbor. The trail goes left and narrows as it approaches the harbor and the crashing surf in the distance.

Head out on a sandy trail on a peninsula toward Dorr Point, but stop before the erosion. Compass Harbor and Ogden Point are located to the left (north and northwest) and Sols Cliff is to the right (southeast). Frenchman Bay is straight ahead. In spring you can find wild lupine and flowering trees near the shore.

Just before reaching the point, an unofficial trail leads to the ruins of the Dorr estate, built on land purchased by his father in 1868 and accepted by the federal government as part of the park in 1942, according to an article in 2004 in *Chebacco,* the magazine of the Mount Desert Island Historical Society.

We counted forty-three granite steps and came upon an aged brick foundation. The Park Service does not maintain the old home site, and there were no historical markers at the time of our visit. None of Dorr's formal gardens remain, but there are many nonnative plants that can still be found at the homesite and in the surrounding forest, some of which may have been among those originally transplanted from the family's Massachusetts estate.

Dorr was adamant that his cherished Old Farm become part of the park, and even offered the property as a summer

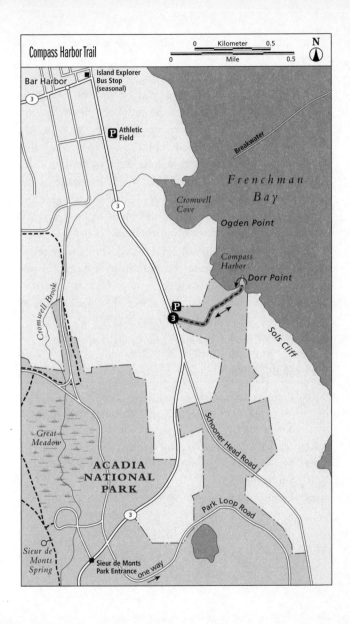

Compass Harbor Trail

Bar Harbor

Island Explorer Bus Stop (seasonal)

Athletic Field

Cromwell Cove

Frenchman Bay

Breakwater

Ogden Point

Compass Harbor

Dorr Point

Sols Cliff

Cromwell Brook

ACADIA NATIONAL PARK

Great Meadow

Schooner Head Road

Park Loop Road

Sieur de Monts Spring

Sieur de Monts Park Entrance

one way

Kilometer

Mile

N

White House to both Presidents Calvin Coolidge and Franklin D. Roosevelt to garner support, according to the 2004 historical society article.

The property finally became part of the park two years before he died, according to the article by Ronald Epp, writer of a biography on Dorr. But after the end of World War II, the federal government found it too expensive to preserve and maintain Old Farm and razed the estate, Epp said.

At that time in the nation's history, in the wake of the Great Depression and World War II, one can imagine the federal government didn't have the funds to keep up Old Farm, or many other facilities or programs.

Today the National Park Service calls Dorr the father of the park and credits him for his indefatigable work in leading the effort to create Acadia.

There's no better spot to ponder that than Compass Harbor.

Return the way you came.

Miles and Directions

0.0 Compass Harbor trailhead, which leaves from the parking lot on the left (east) side of ME 3, just south of Nannau Wood, a private road.

0.1 Turn left at the junction toward Compass Harbor.

0.4 Approach Dorr Point and the remains of George B. Dorr's Old Farm estate.

0.8 Return to the trailhead.

4 Cadillac Summit Loop Trail

Located at the top of Acadia's highest mountain, this short and easy trail offers maybe the best views in the park and plaques that identify more than forty islands, peaks, and other key points that lie off its slopes. On a sunny day this loop is the best place for any hiker to get some bearings before exploring the rest of Acadia. The trail is often busy during peak summer months, since cars and buses can drive up the mountain's access road.

Distance: 0.3-mile loop
Approximate hiking time: 30 minutes
Difficulty: Easy
Trail surface: Paved walkway
Best season: Spring through fall, particularly early morning or late afternoon in the summer to avoid crowds
Other trail users: Hikers coming from Gorge Path or Cadillac North Ridge or Cadillac South Ridge Trails, visitors with wheelchairs or baby strollers, birders

Canine compatibility: Leashed dogs permitted
Map: USGS Acadia National Park and Vicinity
Special considerations: The walkway is also designed to be partially accessible for visitors with wheelchairs or baby strollers. The 3.5-mile paved auto road to the summit is a winding and narrow route. There is a seasonal summit gift shop and restrooms.

Finding the trailhead: From the park visitor center, drive south on the Park Loop Road for about 3.5 miles and turn left (east) at the sign for Cadillac Mountain. Ascend the winding summit road to the top. The paved walkway begins off the eastern side of the parking lot, across from the summit gift shop. The Island Explorer bus does not go up Cadillac, but the Loop Road line has a Cadillac North Ridge stop, where the 2.2-mile moderately difficult Cadillac North Ridge

Trail takes you to the top, and a connection with the Cadillac Summit Loop Trail. **GPS:** N44 35.26' / W068 22.46'

The Hike

You gain a new appreciation for 1,530-foot-high Cadillac Mountain on this trail, with plaques describing the history and features of Mount Desert Island and the spectacular views from Acadia's highest summit.

One display explains the geological essence of Acadia— the pink granite with its three main minerals. Another commemorates Stephen Tyng Mather, a wealthy entrepreneur and leading advocate for creation of the National Park Service in 1916, and the first director of the Park Service. And yet another describes whom the mountain was named for, a seventeenth-century French explorer who also founded Detroit and later became the namesake for the iconic American car.

A top feature of this hike is a circular viewing area with two plaques that pinpoint about forty highlights of the sweeping views, allowing anyone to find spots such as the Turtle Islands, Frenchman Bay, Schoodic Peninsula, Porcupine Islands, Seawall, Baker Island, and the Gulf of Maine.

Aside from the vistas described in the plaques, you may also see bald eagles and turkey vultures soaring above Cadillac, especially during the annual HawkWatch late August through Columbus Day, when migrating raptors such as kestrels, peregrine falcons, and sharp-shinned hawks can be spotted.

There are two access points to the paved summit loop trail off the eastern edge of the parking area, marked by signs on wood posts. The access point on the left (northeast), near the handicapped parking spots, is also the start of a ramp

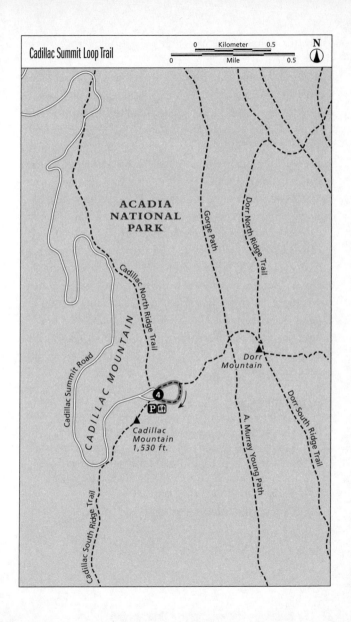

Cadillac Summit Loop Trail

ACADIA
NATIONAL
PARK

Gorge Path

Dorr North Ridge Trail

Cadillac North Ridge Trail

Cadillac Summit Road

CADILLAC MOUNTAIN

Dorr
Mountain

▲ Cadillac
Mountain
1,530 ft.

Dorr South Ridge Trail

A. Murray Young Path

Cadillac South Ridge Trail

N

0   Kilometer   0.5
0   Mile   0.5

for visitors with wheelchairs and baby strollers to reach the accessible circular viewing area.

The trail, originally built by the Civilian Conservation Corps, the Depression-era public work relief program, is tinged to match the pink Cadillac granite and features several sets of granite boulders for steps.

Sheep laurel and other greenery, a tiny white flower known as mountain sandwort, and even a couple of small birch trees line the walkway, proof of the success of restoration efforts over the past decade. Wooden barricades and signs reminding hikers to stay on the trail and solid rock are part of the continued revegetation program.

Because of its grand vistas and easy access, the trail can get very crowded in the summer. Early and late in the day are best. But there can even be small crowds at sunrise, especially at the times of year when the sun's rays first hit the United States atop Cadillac, the eastern seaboard's highest mountain. And there can even be a motor brigade heading up for the sunset, as we found one afternoon as dusk approached.

Miles and Directions

0.0 Cadillac Summit Loop trailhead, with two access points located at the eastern edge of the parking area, across from the summit shop. The left (northeastern) trail entrance connects to a ramp that allows wheelchair and baby stroller access to a circular viewing area.

0.3 Complete the loop at the trailhead.

5 Beachcroft Path

Intricately laid stone steps lead much of the way to open views along Huguenot Head, on the shoulder of Champlain Mountain. In line with its more than century-old history, this route's name is reverting to the original description as a path, rather than a trail, to better characterize its highly constructed nature. It's a mostly moderate ascent to this hike's goal, but there's an option to climb more strenuously for another 0.5 mile to reach the summit of Champlain and its ocean views.

Distance: 1.4 miles out and back

Approximate hiking time: 1 to 1.5 hours

Difficulty: Moderate to more challenging

Trail surface: Granite steps, rock ledges, forest floor

Best season: Spring through fall

Other trail users: None

Canine compatibility: Leashed dogs permitted

Map: USGS Acadia National Park and Vicinity

Special considerations: If you tack on the stretch to the top of Champlain, be aware that the steep section is not recommended for dogs. There are no facilities at the trailhead. Seasonal restrooms are at the nearby Sieur de Monts park entrance.

Finding the trailhead: From downtown Bar Harbor head south on ME 3 for about 2.2 miles, just past the park's Sieur de Monts entrance, to the parking lot on the right (west) just before the glacially carved lake known as the Tarn. The trailhead is on the left (east) side of ME 3, across the road diagonally (southeast) from the parking lot. The closest Island Explorer stop is Sieur de Monts on the Sand Beach and Loop Road lines. **GPS:** N44 35.84' / W068 20.53'

The Hike

The Beachcroft Path climbs to the shoulder of Huguenot Head, with an average elevation gain of 100 feet each tenth of a mile, but at times it feels remarkably like a walk along a garden path. The gradual switchbacks and neatly laid stepping stones turn what would otherwise be a vertical scramble into a gentler ascent.

Adding to the wonder are the constant open views north toward Frenchman Bay, west toward Dorr Mountain, south toward the Cranberry Isles, east toward Champlain Mountain, and down to the Tarn.

The dome-shaped Huguenot Head, visible from Bar Harbor, has been a popular destination for more than a century. The Beachcroft Path, built and rebuilt in the late 1800s and early 1900s, was named for the estate of the Bar Harbor summer resident who financed its construction. It consists of hundreds of hand-hewn stepping-stones and countless switchbacks.

When it was originally constructed by George B. Dorr and the Bar Harbor Village Improvement Association, the path began at Sieur de Monts Spring, but road construction led the path's start to be moved.

From the trailhead across from the Tarn parking area, ascend via the switchbacks and stone steps, catching your breath on the plentiful level sections along the way. But be careful, as even the flattest-looking rock along the path can be loose, and as you travel on open rock ledges.

Near the shoulder of Huguenot Head, the path widens and levels off. It circles to the northeast as you reach the open ledge just below the head's summit, ending at 0.7 mile with views south toward the Cranberry Isles. To the east

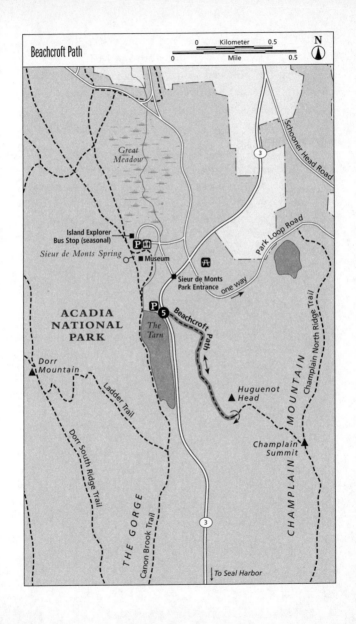

Beachcroft Path

0   Kilometer   0.5

0   Mile   0.5

N

Great Meadow

Schooner Head Road

3

Park Loop Road

Island Explorer
Bus Stop (seasonal)

P

Sieur de Monts Spring

Museum

Sieur de Monts
Park Entrance

one way

ACADIA
NATIONAL
PARK

P 5 Beachcroft Path

The Tarn

*Dorr
Mountain*

Ladder Trail

*Huguenot
Head*

CHAMPLAIN MOUNTAIN

Champlain North Ridge Trail

Dorr South Ridge Trail

*Champlain
Summit*

THE GORGE

Canon Brook Trail

3

To Seal Harbor

(left) is Champlain Mountain, and to the west (right) is Dorr Mountain. Down below are the Tarn and ME 3.

Return the way you came, although ambitious hikers can continue east toward Champlain Mountain, a more challenging additional 0.5-mile climb.

Miles and Directions

0.0   Beachcroft Path trailhead, diagonally (southeast) across ME 3 from the parking lot that's just south of the Sieur de Monts park entrance.

0.7   Reach the open ledge on the shoulder of Huguenot Head with views.

1.4   Return to the trailhead.

6 Champlain North Ridge Trail (Bear Brook Trail)

Enjoy expansive views from the summit of Champlain Mountain and all along the open ridge, the closest to the ocean of all of Acadia's ridges. At times you'll see the contrast of fog rolling in over Frenchman Bay below and sun shining overhead, or storm clouds streaming in from the west as clear skies still prevail to the east.

Distance: 2.0 miles out and back

Approximate hiking time: 1.5 to 2 hours

Difficulty: Moderate to more challenging

Trail surface: Rock ledges, forest floor

Best season: Spring through fall

Other trail users: None

Canine compatibility: Leashed dogs permitted

Map: USGS Acadia National Park and Vicinity

Special considerations: No facilities at trailhead; seasonal restrooms at nearby Bear Brook picnic area

Finding the trailhead: Enter the park at the Sieur de Monts entrance, which is about 2 miles south of downtown Bar Harbor on ME 3. Turn right (south) on the one-way Park Loop Road. The trailhead is 0.8 mile from the entrance, on the right (south) after the Bear Brook picnic area. There is a small parking area on the left (north), across the road just beyond the trailhead. The closest Island Explorer stop is Sieur de Monts on the Loop Road and Sand Beach lines, but it's a bit of a walk, so you may want to ask if the bus driver can let you off at the trailhead. **GPS:** N44 36.28' / W068 19.44'

The Hike

On the Champlain North Ridge Trail early one morning, a blanket of fog enveloped the Porcupine Islands in the space of a few minutes. Amazingly, the ridgetop trail continued to be bathed in sunshine as the foghorns sounded their warnings below.

Another time, we started a late afternoon walk under sunny skies, but by the time we got to the summit a mile away, strong rain forced us to put on full storm gear from head to toe. It was sunny once again as we returned to the trailhead.

Contrasts like these are part of the very nature of Acadia, where the mountains meet the sea and the weather can vary from moment to moment.

The trail, recently renamed as part of a multiyear effort to update some of the park's historic routes, offers spectacular views from Frenchman Bay to Great Head as it climbs the northern ridge of 1,058-foot Champlain Mountain.

This is one of the oldest marked trails on Mount Desert Island, showing up on 1890s maps, when Champlain used to be known as Newport Mountain.

From the trailhead head south and start ascending through a birch grove. The trail levels off a bit at about 0.2 mile and then ascends more steeply up some stone steps.

The junction with the Orange & Black Path (formerly known as the East Face Trail) is at 0.4 mile. Continue straight (south), and climb a steep pink-granite face. Follow blue blazes and Bates-style cairns, which are artfully placed groups of four to six rocks that point the way, as you near the summit.

As part of staying true to the history of Acadia's trails, the Bates cairns, pioneered by Waldron Bates, chair of the Roads

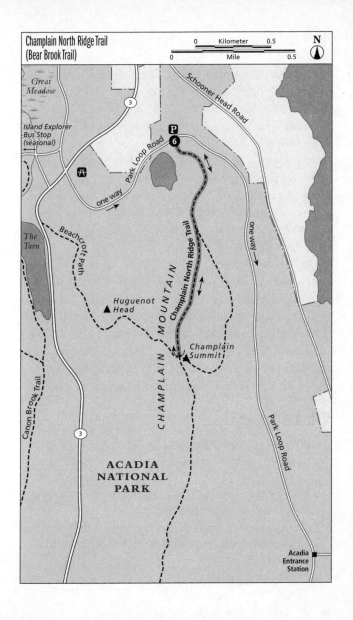

Champlain North Ridge Trail
(Bear Brook Trail)

| Kilometer | 0 | | 0.5 |
| Mile | 0 | | 0.5 |

N

Great
Meadow

3

Schooner Head Road

Island Explorer
Bus Stop
(seasonal)

P
6

Park Loop Road

one way

The
Tarn

Beachcroft Path

Huguenot
Head

C H A M P L A I N   M O U N T A I N

Champlain North Ridge Trail

one way

Champlain
Summit

Canon Brook Trail

3

Park Loop Road

ACADIA
NATIONAL
PARK

Acadia
Entrance
Station

and Paths Committee of the Bar Harbor Village Improvement Association from 1900 to 1909, have replaced conical piles of rocks and supplement blue blazes as trail markers, particularly on ridgelines on the east side of Mount Desert Island. But don't be tempted to move, add, or take away rocks from the seemingly Zen-like Bates cairns, cautions Charlie Jacobi, Acadia natural resource specialist. That's because they're designed with a purpose, with the gap in the base and the top stone pointing in the right direction. Any alteration can wreak havoc for other hikers, never mind for those who maintain the trails. "It's part of the leave-no-trace principle," says Jacobi. And it's also part of respecting history, with some Bates cairns dating back a century.

At 1.0 mile reach the Champlain summit, with the closest mountaintop views of Frenchman Bay and the Porcupine Islands in all of Acadia. You also reach the junction with the Precipice and Champlain South Ridge Trails and the upper Beachcroft Path at the summit.

Return the way you came, although intrepid hikers can continue down the Champlain South Ridge Trail for another 1.6 miles to a mountain pond known as the Bowl.

Miles and Directions

0.0 Champlain North Ridge trailhead, on the right (south) side of the one-way Park Loop Road, after the Bear Brook picnic area.

0.4 Reach the junction with the Orange & Black Path. Bear right and continue on the main trail.

1.0 Arrive at the Champlain Mountain summit and the junction with the Precipice and Champlain South Ridge Trails and the upper Beachcroft Path.

2.0 Return to the trailhead.

7 Murphy Lane to Schooner Head Path and Overlook

Sample a unique Acadia experience by walking along recently reopened historic trails from the base of Champlain's cliffs to a spectacular shore overlook. Along the way you'll pass through deciduous forest and by a pond with grand cliff views, and you can imagine what it was like when nineteenth-century rusticators traveled these same footpaths.

Distance: 2.0 miles out and back

Approximate hiking time: 1 to 1.5 hours

Difficulty: Easy

Trail surface: Forest floor, graded gravel path, wooden bridge

Best season: Spring through fall

Other trail users: Joggers, dog walkers, area residents

Canine compatibility: Leashed dogs permitted

Map: USGS Acadia National Park and Vicinity

Special considerations: No facilities at trailhead

Finding the trailhead: Enter the park at the Sieur de Monts entrance, which is about 2 miles south of downtown Bar Harbor on ME 3. Turn right (south) on the one-way Park Loop Road. The trailhead is 2 miles from the entrance, on the left (east), diagonally across the Park Loop Road from the Precipice parking area. The closest Island Explorer stop is Sieur de Monts on the Loop Road and Sand Beach lines, but you'll want to ask if the bus driver can let you off at the Precipice parking area. **GPS:** N44 34.85' / W068 18.74'

The Hike

If you find the Precipice Trail closed during peregrine falcon nesting season, don't be disappointed. Instead you can use the same jumping-off point at the foot of Champlain Mountain to explore recently reopened historic routes, taking you through the woods and down to the ocean.

Where else but in Acadia can you go from cliff to shore in just a mile? And also step through time?

The recently reopened Murphy Lane, once open to horses and known as the Blue Path, appeared on maps dating back to the 1890s, according to *Pathmakers: Cultural Landscape Report for the Historic Hiking Trail System of Mount Desert Island*, by the National Park Service's Olmsted Center for Landscape Preservation.

From the Murphy Lane trailhead across the Park Loop Road from the Precipice parking area, head into the woods on a trail that's level and smooth enough to jog. Stay straight and don't be confused by old woods paths that may crisscross in spots.

In 0.3 mile you'll come to Schooner Head Path, a recently reopened historic route that once allowed nineteenth-century rusticators, or artists and other city folks who summered in Bar Harbor and lived like the locals, to walk from the village all the way down to Sand Beach and other points. Turn right on the graded gravel path and head southeast, paralleling Schooner Head Road.

(You'll travel along only a portion of Schooner Head Path for this hike, but you can still imagine yourself a modern-day rusticator, seeing some of the same views that Hudson River School artists like Thomas Cole and Frederic Church saw, or that George B. Dorr, regarded as the father of Acadia National Park, fought so hard to protect. The path, first built in 1901, recently reopened with funds from the Acadia Trails Forever initiative and the private Fore River Foundation, and is a cooperative effort of the Park Service, Friends of Acadia, area residents, the town of Bar Harbor, and nearby Jackson Laboratory.)

At 0.8 mile Schooner Head Path takes you over a wooden bridge built over the outlet of a pond, where you can look back at the grand view of the Champlain cliffs, the start of the hike.

The path soon bears right, winding its way through hilly woods, before coming back out to the road again at 0.9 mile. Cross the road and enter the woods again on the other side. The path becomes a bit hillier.

At 1.0 mile you'll reach the parking area for Schooner Head Overlook. Turn left along the paved parking lot road over to the shorefront views. To the north (left) is the rocky peninsula known as Schooner Head, and out in Frenchman Bay is Egg Rock, with its lighthouse.

Return the way you came.

Miles and Directions

0.0   Murphy Lane trailhead, across the one-way Park Loop Road from the Precipice parking area.

0.3   Reach the junction with Schooner Head Path. Turn right onto the graded gravel path that parallels Schooner Head Road.

0.8   Cross a wooden bridge over the outlet of a pond, with views back toward the Champlain cliffs.

0.9   Cross Schooner Head Road and head back into the woods.

1.0   Reach Schooner Head Overlook and turn left along the paved parking lot road for shorefront views.

2.0   Return to the trailhead.

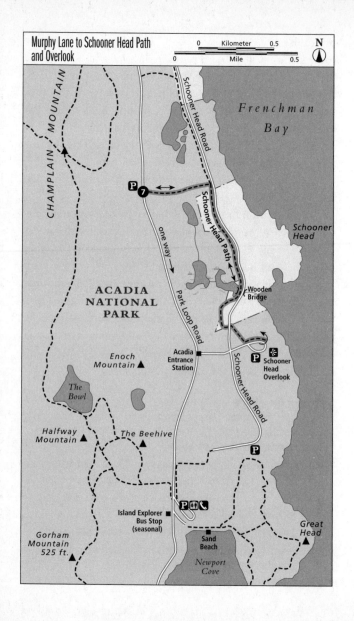

Kilometer

Mile

N

Frenchman Bay

Schooner Head Road

P 7

Schooner Head Path

Schooner Head

CHAMPLAIN MOUNTAIN

one way

Park Loop Road

ACADIA NATIONAL PARK

Wooden Bridge

Enoch Mountain ▲

Acadia Entrance Station

Schooner Head Road

P Schooner Head Overlook

The Bowl

Halfway Mountain ▲

The Beehive ▲

P

P 📶 📞

Island Explorer Bus Stop (seasonal)

Gorham Mountain 525 ft. ▲

Sand Beach

Great Head ▲

Newport Cove

Options

If you'd rather hike in reverse, for a shore-to-cliff experience, you can drive down Schooner Head Road to Schooner Head Overlook, park, and take Schooner Head Path to Murphy Lane to the Precipice parking area. Or you can take the Island Explorer's Loop Road or Sand Beach line and ask to be let off at the Park Loop Road entrance station. Follow the paved connector road east from the park entrance station out to Schooner Head Overlook, and hike in reverse.

You can also explore more of Schooner Head Path, by adding on a newly reopened connector to the Orange & Black Path, about 0.5 mile northwest of the junction with Murphy Lane, or by following Schooner Head Path northwest and then north by northeast all the way to Compass Harbor on the outskirts of Bar Harbor. Some parts of the northern section of Schooner Head Path cross private property, so be respectful of property owners' rights and stay on the established route.

8 Sand Beach and Great Head Trail

Enjoy Acadia's only ocean beach, made of sand, tiny shell fragments, quartz, and pink feldspar. Then take a hike along the Great Head Trail for its expansive views of the Beehive, Champlain Mountain, Otter Cliff, Egg Rock, and the Cranberry Isles. Also visible just off the tip of Great Head peninsula is an unusual rock formation called Old Soaker.

Distance: 1.5-mile lollipop
Approximate hiking time: 1 to 1.5 hours
Difficulty: Moderate
Trail surface: Beach, rock ledges, forest floor
Best season: Spring through fall, particularly early morning or late afternoon in the summer to avoid the beach crowds
Other trail users: Sunbathers on Sand Beach in summertime
Canine compatibility: Dogs prohibited on Sand Beach from May 15 through Sept 15; leashed dogs permitted other times of year
Map: USGS Acadia National Park and Vicinity
Special considerations: Seasonal restrooms and changing area and a pay phone are available at the Sand Beach parking lot; bring extra socks or a towel in case your feet get wet when you cross a small channel to get from the beach to the trailhead

Finding the trailhead: From the park's visitor center, drive south on the Park Loop Road for about 3 miles and turn left (east) at the sign for Sand Beach. Follow the one-way Park Loop Road for about 5.5 miles, past the park fee station, to the beach parking lot on the left (east) side of the road. The Island Explorer's Loop Road and Sand Beach lines stop at the beach parking lot. Walk down the stairs at the eastern end of the parking lot and head east across Sand Beach to the Great head trailhead. **GPS:** N44 32.95' / W068 18.36'

The Hike

A hike on the Great Head peninsula is a perfect way to break up a lazy summer afternoon lounging on Sand Beach.

A relatively modest scramble up the rocky slope of Great Head leads you to dramatic views of the beach you just left behind, as well as vistas of such other notable park features as the Beehive, Champlain Mountain, and Otter Cliff.

Once, when we hiked Great Head with our nieces Sharon and Michelle, the views were made even more dramatic by the fog that first enveloped Sand Beach and the Beehive behind us, and then receded like the outgoing tide.

"I feel like I'm living in a postcard," said Sharon, fifteen at the time.

"This is really fun," said Michelle, twelve at the time, as opposed to the "kind of fun" rating she'd given to a hike with less dramatic views that we'd done the day before.

Since the 1840s and 1850s, Great Head has been a popular destination for artists and tourists. A stone teahouse, known as Satterlee's Tower, once stood on the summit, and the ruins of it are still visible.

Today, during the busy summer season, you may see boaters coming close to the Great Head cliffs or rock climbers scaling them.

To get to the trailhead from the parking lot, head down the stairs to the beach and travel to the farthest (easternmost) end. Cross a channel—best at low tide to keep your feet dry—to the Great Head trailhead.

Go up a series of granite steps bordered by a split-rail fence. At the top of the steps, at 0.1 mile, turn right (southeast) and follow the blue blazes and cairns up the rocky ledges. Views of Sand Beach, the Beehive, and Champlain Mountain are immediately visible.

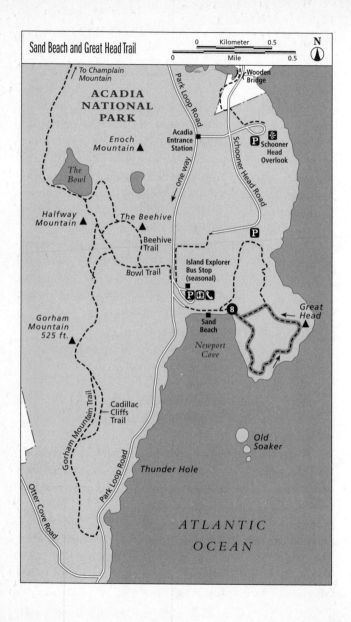

Sand Beach and Great Head Trail

Kilometer 0   0.5
Mile   0   0.5

N

To Champlain Mountain

ACADIA NATIONAL PARK

Park Loop Road

Wooden Bridge

Enoch Mountain ▲

The Bowl

Acadia Entrance Station

Schooner Head Road

Schooner Head Overlook

one way

P

Halfway Mountain ▲

The Beehive ▲

Beehive Trail

P

Bowl Trail

Island Explorer Bus Stop (seasonal)

P

Gorham Mountain 525 ft. ▲

8

Great Head ▲

Sand Beach

Newport Cove

Cadillac Cliffs Trail

Gorham Mountain Trail

Old Soaker

Thunder Hole

Park Loop Road

Otter Cove Road

ATLANTIC OCEAN

At the next trail junction, at about 0.2 mile, bear right (south) to head toward the tip of the peninsula, with views of rectangular-shaped Old Soaker nearby and Otter Cliff and the Cranberry Isles in the distance.

At 0.5 mile the trail rounds the peninsula. At 0.8 mile it reaches the summit of Great Head, where there are views of Frenchman Bay and Egg Rock.

At about 1.1 miles, along a level section of the trail, you will reach a junction in a birch grove. Turn left (southwest) and ascend gradually up Great Head ridge, with views of Champlain Mountain, the Beehive, and Gorham Mountain. (If you go straight (northwest) at this junction to a parking lot near Schooner Head Road instead, and then circle back, you can add another 0.8 mile to the loop.)

At the last junction, at 1.3 miles, bear right (northwest) to return to the trailhead and Sand Beach, for a loop hike of 1.5 miles.

Miles and Directions

0.0   Begin at the Great Head trailhead, which is at the east end of Sand Beach.

0.1   Bear right (southeast) at the top of the stairs.

0.2   At the junction with the spur trail inland, go right (south) along the shore.

0.5   Reach the south end of the Great Head peninsula and follow the trail as it curves northeast along the shore.

0.8   Arrive on the Great Head summit, where the remnants of a stone teahouse can be found.

1.1   At the junction in the birch grove with the spur trail to Great Head ridge, bear left (southwest).

1.3   Bear right (northwest) at the junction.

1.5   Return to the trailhead, completing the loop.

9 Ocean Path

This easy hike takes you along Acadia's distinct pink granite coastline, bringing you to Thunder Hole, where you may hear a reverberating boom as the surf crashes against the shore; Otter Cliff, where you may see rock climbers on the 60-foot precipice; and Otter Point, where you may catch a colorful sunset.

Distance: 4.0 miles out and back

Approximate hiking time: 2 to 2.5 hours

Difficulty: Easy

Trail surface: Graded gravel path, forest floor

Best season: Spring through fall, particularly early morning or late afternoon in the summer to avoid the crowds

Other trail users: Motorists who stop along the Park Loop Road to view Thunder Hole or Otter Point, rock climbers accessing Otter Cliff

Canine compatibility: Leashed dogs permitted

Map: USGS Acadia National Park and Vicinity

Special considerations: Seasonal restrooms and a pay phone available at Sand Beach parking lot; seasonal restrooms at Thunder Hole and Fabbri parking areas

Finding the trailhead: From the park's visitor center, drive south on the Park Loop Road for about 3 miles and turn left (east) at the sign for Sand Beach. Follow the one-way Park Loop Road for about 5.5 miles, past the park fee station, to the beach parking lot on the left (east) side of the road. The trailhead is on the right (east) just before the stairs to the beach. The Island Explorer bus's Loop Road and Sand Beach lines stop at the beach parking lot. **GPS:** N44 32.94' / W068 18.38'

The Hike

The sounds of the ocean and the views of rocky cliffs and pink granite shoreline are never far from Ocean Path. At Thunder Hole, halfway along the path, when the conditions are just right, the surf crashes through rocky chasms with a thunderous roar. And at Otter Point, at trail's end, the sound of a buoy ringing fills the air. Rock climbers can be seen scaling Otter Cliff, one of the premier rock climbing areas in the eastern United States, while picnickers, birders, and sun worshippers can be found enjoying themselves on the flat pink granite slabs that dot the shore here.

First used as a buckboard road in the 1870s, Ocean Path and Ocean Drive were incorporated into John D. Rockefeller Jr.'s vision of scenic roads, bringing visitors to many of Mount Desert Island's unique features. He began motor road construction in the park in 1927 and hired landscape architect Frederick Law Olmsted Jr. to lay out many of the routes, including the Otter Cliff section of Ocean Drive. Ocean Path was rebuilt during the Great Depression of the 1930s by the Civilian Conservation Corps, with funding assistance from Rockefeller.

Because of its ease and accessibility, Ocean Path can be crowded during the height of the tourist season. The best time to walk it is either very early or very late on a summer's day, or in the spring or fall as we have.

The Ocean Path trailhead is on the right just before the stairs to Sand Beach. Follow the gravel path past the changing rooms and restrooms, up a series of stairs, and then left (south) away from a secondary parking area. The easy trail takes you southwest along the shore, paralleling the Ocean Drive section of the Park Loop Road.

Thunder Hole, a popular destination, is at 1.0 mile. Many visitors driving through the park on calm summer days stop here and cause a traffic jam but go away disappointed. It turns out the best time to experience the power of Thunder Hole is after a storm and as high tide approaches, when the surf crashes violently through the chasms, pushing trapped air against the rock and creating a sound like the clap of thunder.

But even when you know the best time to hear Thunder Hole, it can still take a number of times before you hit it right. On one trip to Acadia, we went with our nieces Sharon and Michelle to this spot three times, once late at night with stormy seas, but didn't hear the thundering boom as we expected.

If you, too, find yourself coming to Thunder Hole during stormy conditions, be careful. Visitors have been swept out to sea here and at Schoodic Peninsula, a reminder of how powerful nature can be along Acadia's coast. Watch out for large waves, stay a safe distance away, and don't turn your back on the ocean.

At 1.3 miles on Ocean Path, you will pass a short series of stairs on the right (west), which lead you across the Park Loop Road to the Gorham Mountain trailhead.

The path's only noticeable elevation gain comes as it rises through the woods toward Otter Cliff, reached at 1.8 miles. On the approach, rock climbers can be seen scaling the rock face or waiting at the top of the cliffs for their turn. A staircase leads down on the left (east) to the rock climbers' registration board.

Ocean Path ends at 2.0 miles, at Otter Point, where you can watch the sun set over Acadia and find a nearby commemorative plaque dedicated to Rockefeller.

Return the way you came.

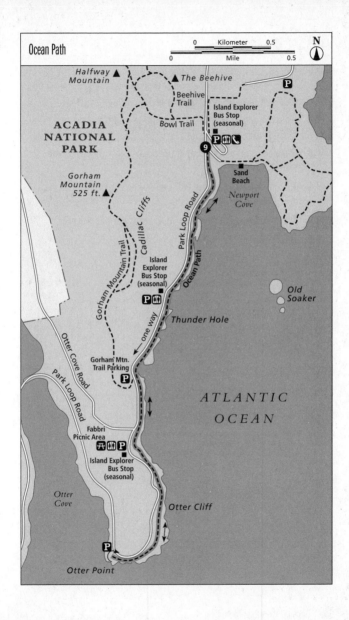

Miles and Directions

0.0 Ocean Path trailhead, on the right just before the stairs to Sand Beach. Follow the gravel path up a series of stairs and then left (south) away from a secondary parking area.

1.0 Reach Thunder Hole, where a viewing platform may be closed during stormy seas.

1.3 Pass the Gorham Mountain trailhead, which is across the Park Loop Road.

1.8 Reach Otter Cliff, where you can see rock climbers scaling the precipice.

2.0 Arrive at Otter Point, where you can watch the sun set.

4.0 Return to the trailhead.

10 The Bowl Trail

This hike leads to a mountain pond called the Bowl, where you can encounter wildlife, especially if you travel early in the morning or late in the afternoon. You can connect to the Gorham Mountain and Champlain South Ridge Trails off this trail. And you can find more moderate ascents up the back side of the nearby Beehive, a nice alternative to climbing the iron ladder rungs up that peak's cliff.

Distance: 1.4 miles out and back

Approximate hiking time: 1 to 1.5 hours

Difficulty: Moderate

Trail surface: Forest floor, rock ledges

Best season: Spring through fall, particularly early morning or late afternoon in the summer to avoid the crowds

Other trail users: Hikers climbing the Beehive

Canine compatibility: Leashed dogs permitted (but not on the ladder climb up the Beehive)

Map: USGS Acadia National Park and Vicinity

Special considerations: Seasonal restrooms and a pay phone at Sand Beach parking lot

Finding the trailhead: From the park's visitor center, drive south on the Park Loop Road for about 3 miles and turn left (east) at the sign for Sand Beach. Follow the one-way Park Loop Road for about 5.5 miles, past the park fee station, to the beach parking lot on the left (east) side of the road. The Island Explorer's Loop Road and Sand Beach lines stop at the beach parking lot. The trailhead is diagonally (northwest) across the Park Loop Road from the beach parking lot. **GPS:** N44 33.17' / W068 18.53'

The Hike

Views of a great blue heron taking off low across the water's surface or of a turkey vulture soaring high on the thermals are among the possible rewards when you hike to the Bowl, a mountain pond at more than 400 feet in elevation.

We got lucky and got both views in the same day as we hiked along the shoreline.

Another time, during a walk down from the Bowl, we heard a loud snorting in the woods. A couple of white-tailed deer darted through the trees, the snorting apparently an alarm call.

Hike in the early morning or late afternoon to improve your chances of such wildlife encounters.

The Bowl Trail begins by climbing gradually through lowland birch forest, passing junctions with the very steep Beehive Trail, featuring iron ladder rungs, at 0.2 mile; a spur to the Gorham Mountain Trail at 0.4 mile; another spur to the Beehive at 0.5 mile that's a more gradual alternative to the ladder approach; and the Gorham Mountain Trail at 0.6 mile.

Beyond, the Bowl Trail heads up steeply through the woods, then goes downhill, arriving at the Bowl at the 0.7-mile mark. This also marks the junction with the 1.6-mile Champlain South Ridge Trail, which heads left (northwest), and another moderate spur to the Beehive, which heads right (east).

Return the way you came.

Miles and Directions

0.0 Bowl trailhead, diagonally (northwest) across the Park Loop Road from the Sand Beach parking lot.

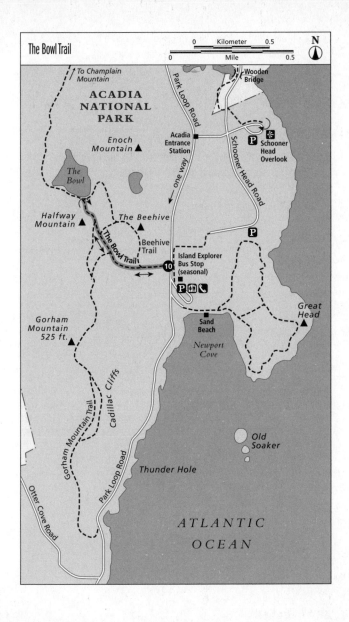

0.2 Reach the junction with the Beehive Trail, a very steep ladder climb that heads right, up that peak's cliff.

0.4 A spur trail to the Gorham Mountain Trail heads left at this junction.

0.5 A more moderate spur trail up the Beehive heads right at this junction.

0.6 The Gorham Mountain Trail heads left at this junction.

0.7 Arrive at the Bowl and the junction with the Champlain South Ridge Trail and another moderate spur trail up the Beehive.

1.4 Return to the trailhead.

11 Gorham Mountain Trail

This is a classic Acadia hike to a 525-foot peak with sweeping views of Great Head, Sand Beach, Otter Cliff, Champlain Mountain, and the Beehive. The trail, among the most traveled in the park, is also one of the most historic, dating back to the early 1900s and the Great Depression. The hike includes a spur trail to Cadillac Cliffs and an ancient sea cave.

Distance: 1.8 miles out and back

Approximate hiking time: 1 to 1.5 hours

Difficulty: Moderate

Trail surface: Forest floor, rock ledges

Best season: Spring to fall, particularly early morning or late afternoon in the summer to avoid crowds

Other trail users: None

Canine compatibility: Leashed dogs permitted (but not recommended on the optional Cadillac Cliffs Trail, which features a couple of iron rungs)

Map: USGS Acadia National Park and Vicinity

Special considerations: No facilities at trailhead, but nearby seasonal restrooms at Thunder Hole and Fabbri parking areas

Finding the trailhead: From the park's visitor center, drive south on the Park Loop Road for about 3 miles, and turn left (east) at the sign for Sand Beach. Follow the one-way Park Loop Road for about 7 miles, passing the park fee station, Sand Beach, and Thunder Hole, to the Gorham Mountain sign and parking lot. **GPS:** N44 31.69' / W068 19.12'

The Hike

The Gorham Mountain Trail, marked by blue blazes and historic Bates-style cairns, takes hikers to some of the most rewarding views in Acadia, with nearly uninterrupted ridgetop panoramas of everything from Great Head and Sand Beach to the Beehive, from Cadillac to Dorr Mountain. The trail follows the great ridge that runs north all the way to Champlain Mountain and is the closest to the ocean of all of Acadia's mountain ridges.

An additional bonus, if you choose to take it, is the 0.5-mile spur trail to the once-submerged Cadillac Cliffs and an ancient sea cave, which illustrates the powerful geologic forces that helped shape Mount Desert Island.

From the Gorham Mountain parking lot, climb gradually through an evergreen forest and up open ledges, heading north. Though the trail is often shaded by conifers, the sounds of the ocean and the bells of a buoy signal that the shore is nearby. Bunchberry was also blooming during our hike one late spring day.

At 0.2 mile the Cadillac Cliffs Trail leads right (northeast), paralleling and then rejoining the Gorham Mountain Trail at 0.5 mile. Don't miss a plaque at this intersection for Waldron Bates, chair of the Roads and Paths Committee of the Bar Harbor Village Improvement Association from 1900 to 1909, who developed a basic and historic style of cairn now used to mark many Acadia trails, particularly on the east side of the park.

If you want to add the Cadillac Cliffs spur, it is best to do it on the ascent rather than the descent, because of the iron rungs and steep rock face along the way.

Continue on the Gorham Mountain Trail as it moderately ascends the ridge. All along this portion of the route you will enjoy views south to Otter Cliff, east to Great Head and Sand Beach, and north to the Beehive and Champlain Mountain. Frenchman Bay and Egg Rock are also in the distance.

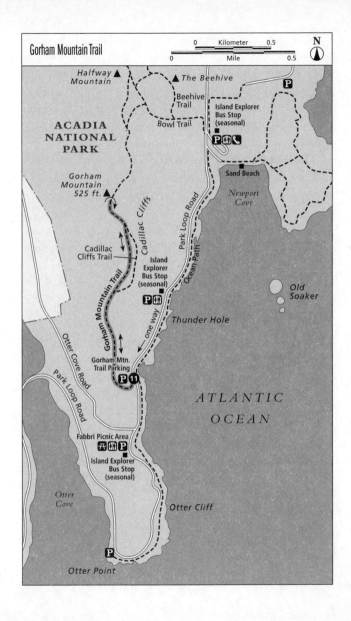

You will even find Bates-style cairns along here, with their four or six stones placed just so, with the opening at the base and the top pointer stone guiding the way. But remember the rules of the trail, and do not add to, take away from, or otherwise alter the cairns that help guide hikers. Two signs, near the beginning of the trail and at the summit, serve as a reminder to leave the cairns untouched.

The summit of Gorham Mountain, at 525 feet, is at 0.9 mile. From here you can barely see Huguenot Head, but it's easy to spot Dorr Mountain between Champlain and Cadillac Mountains.

Return the way you came, although hardy hikers can continue on the trail for another 0.5 mile to a junction with the Bowl Trail and add on the Bowl, the Beehive, or a loop back on Ocean Path.

Miles and Directions

0.0 Gorham Mountain trailhead, which leaves from a parking lot on the right (west) side of the one-way Park Loop Road.

0.2 Reach the junction with the southern end of the Cadillac Cliffs Trail. Stay straight to continue on the trail.

0.5 Pass the junction with the northern end of the Cadillac Cliffs Trail, which comes in from the right (east).

0.9 Arrive on the Gorham Mountain summit.

1.8 Return to the trailhead.

12 Jordan Pond Nature Trail

This short interpretive nature trail leads through woods and along Jordan Pond, bringing you by some of the unique views that Acadia is known for. A brochure is available, describing the evidence still visible from the 1947 fire that burned much of Acadia and Bar Harbor and other aspects of the area's natural and human history.

Distance: 0.5-mile loop
Approximate hiking time: 30 minutes
Difficulty: Easy
Trail surface: Graded gravel path
Best season: Spring through fall, particularly early morning or late afternoon in the summer to avoid the crowds
Other trail users: Motorists using the Jordan Pond boat ramp road that crosses the trail to unload their canoes or kayaks, hikers along the nearby Jordan Pond Path, people walking their bikes to the nearby Jordan Pond House
Canine compatibility: Leashed dogs permitted on the trail, but not in Jordan Pond
Map: USGS Acadia National Park and Vicinity
Special considerations: Accessible to visitors with wheelchairs or baby strollers; chemical toilet at trailhead; full facilities available seasonally at nearby Jordan Pond House

Finding the trailhead: From the park's visitor center, head south on the two-way Park Loop Road for about 7.6 miles and turn right (north) into the Jordan Pond north lot. Park in the lot on the right. The trailhead is at the far end of the lot, at the top of the boat ramp road and on the right (northeast). The Island Explorer's Loop Road and Jordan Pond lines stop at the nearby Jordan Pond House. **GPS:** N44 32.24' / W068 25.28'

The Hike

A lot is packed into this short interpretive trail: panoramic views of Jordan Pond and the distinctive Bubbles on its far shore, and lessons in history and nature. But because it is so accessible, be prepared for the trail to be packed with people during the height of the summer season.

The trail begins in the woods, heading right (northeast) at the top of the boat ramp road. A descriptive brochure is available for purchase for 50 cents, or you can borrow one from the box provided and return it at trail's end.

The first two numbered trail posts take you through deep forests of balsam fir and red spruce, then under broad-leafed American beeches and towering northern white cedars.

At 0.2 mile and trail post 3, as you approach the shore of Jordan Pond, explore the stone walk to the right to get pond and wetland views. The rock path was originally built in the early 1900s and is also part of the Jordan Pond Path, which takes you 3.2 miles around the pond.

Turn around to head back northwest along the nature trail, keeping the pond on your right.

At post 6 you get a lesson in the geology and history of Acadia, with the brochure describing the special granite found here and the dramatic scenery that has attracted artists since the 1840s.

Cross the foot of the boat ramp road after post 7 at 0.3 mile.

At post 8 a plaque describes the power of glaciers in shaping Acadia. Sit awhile here at a commemorative stone bench that looks over Jordan Pond and the twin mountains known as the Bubbles. You can see why Sarah Eliza

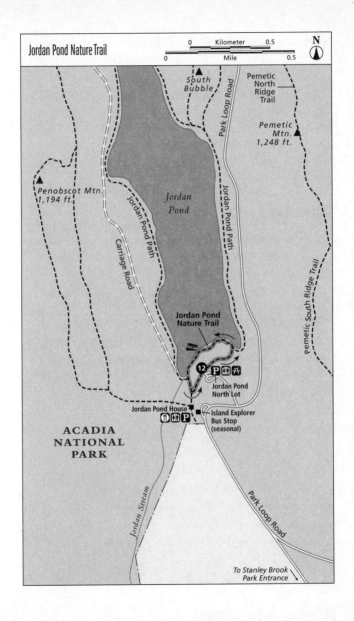

Sigourney Cushing, 1832-1915, in whose memory the bench is dedicated, "dearly loved this spot."

Then, at 0.4 mile, bear left at the fork after post 8 and head back into the woods to post 9. Here the brochure describes how the Jordan Pond House tradition of afternoon tea and popovers came into being around 1900. Bear left again at post 9 to circle back to the parking lot, or if the hike has made you hungry, bear right at post 9 for a short stroll to the Jordan Pond House.

Miles and Directions

0.0 Jordan Pond Nature trailhead, which begins at the top of the boat ramp road at the far end of the Jordan Pond north parking lot, heading right (northeast) into the woods.

0.2 Bear left (northwest), after trail post 3, at the shore of Jordan Pond and the junction with the Jordan Pond Path.

0.3 Cross the foot of the boat ramp road after trail post 7.

0.4 Bear left twice, at the fork after post 8 and after post 9.

0.5 Return to the trailhead, completing the loop.

13 Jordan Pond Path (Jordan Pond Shore Trail)

On this hike you will have expansive views of Jordan Pond, the Bubbles, and Jordan Cliffs, as well as a chance to glimpse a colorful merganser duck or watch kayakers plying the waters. The graded gravel path on the east side of the pond is particularly easy, and an amazing 4,000 feet of log bridges on the west side helps smooth the way over what would otherwise be a potentially wet, rocky, and root-filled trail.

Distance: 3.3-mile loop
Approximate hiking time: 1.5 to 2 hours
Difficulty: Easy
Trail surface: Graded gravel path, rock slabs, forest floor, log bridges, log boardwalk
Best season: Spring through fall, particularly early morning or late afternoon in the summer to avoid the crowds
Other trail users: Motorists using the Jordan Pond boat ramp road that crosses the trail to unload their canoes or kayaks, hikers along the nearby Jordan Pond Nature Trail, people walking their bikes to the nearby Jordan Pond House
Canine compatibility: Leashed dogs permitted on the trail, but not in Jordan Pond
Map: USGS Acadia National Park and Vicinity
Special considerations: Certain sections of graded gravel path on east, west, and south sides of pond accessible to wheelchairs and baby strollers; chemical toilet at trailhead; full facilities available seasonally at nearby Jordan Pond House

Finding the trailhead: From the park's visitor center, head south on the Park Loop Road for about 7.6 miles and turn right (north) into the Jordan Pond north lot. Park in the lot on the right. Follow the boat ramp road down to the shore of the pond (don't take the Jordan Pond Nature Trail at the top of the ramp road that leads into the woods). The trailhead is on the right (east) and leads around the pond. The Island Explorer's Loop Road and Jordan Pond lines stop at the nearby Jordan Pond House. **GPS:** N44 32.27' / W068 25.35'

The Hike

A vigorous walk around Jordan Pond, capped by afternoon tea and popovers on the lawn of the Jordan Pond House—it's one of those special Acadia experiences.

The trail starts from the end of the boat ramp road at the Jordan Pond parking lot and immediately offers a spectacular view of the rounded mountains known as the Bubbles, which lie north across the pond. Bear right (east), circling the pond counterclockwise.

The first half of the trail is along the easy eastern shore with its graded gravel path, but be prepared for the western shore's rock slabs and long series of log bridges known as a bogwalk. The rocks and log bridges can be slippery when wet. Wear proper footwear.

At 0.2 mile you will reach the first of several trails that diverge from the Jordan Pond Path. Bear left, paralleling the shore at each of the junctions. The trail rounds a bend at the south end of the pond, across a rock path that was originally built in the early 1900s, providing pond and wetlands views.

At 0.3 mile pass the junction with the Bubble and Jordan Ponds Path (Pond Trail), which leads to trails up Pemetic Mountain. Stay along the eastern shore of the pond.

The trail now begins heading north. You will soon start seeing Jordan Cliffs to the west across the pond. There are plenty of boulders along the shore to sit on and admire the crystal-clear waters and the tremendous views. Jordan Pond serves as a public water supply, so no swimming is allowed.

After passing over a series of wood bridges, you will soon come up under the towering pinkish granite of South Bubble near the north side of the pond.

At 1.1 miles you will reach Jordan Pond Carry and the South Bubble Trail, which veer to the right (north) and lead, respectively, to Eagle Lake and South Bubble.

At 1.6 miles pass the junction with Bubbles Divide, a trail that heads right (east) up the gap between North and South Bubbles and allows access to the precariously perched Bubble Rock, which is visible from the Park Loop Road.

You are now at the northernmost end of the pond and can get good views of the Jordan Pond House to the south and the Bubbles to the east. Cross a series of intricate wood bridges—one rustic-style span has an archway in the middle.

At 1.7 miles pass the junction with the Deer Brook Trail, which leads up toward Penobscot Mountain and provides access to the Jordan Cliffs Trail and the beautiful double-arch Deer Brook Bridge, built in 1925 as part of the carriage road system.

Now begins the trail's traverse of the rougher western shore of the pond, with its rock slabs and long series of log bridges. After a bit of hide-and-seek with the shore and a stretch of rock hopping, you will reach the log bridges that take you over fragile wetlands.

In addition to the dramatic views of the Bubbles, you may also catch a glimpse of a flock of seagulls or a common merganser, as we did. It is hard to miss a merganser, especially a female, with its rust-colored, crested head and orange bill.

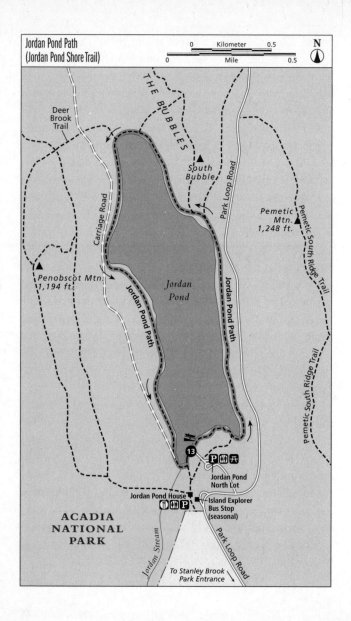

At 3.2 miles turn left on the carriage road and cross a carriage road bridge. Then turn left again to follow the trail as
it circles back to the Jordan Pond north lot at 3.3 miles. Just
before you get back to the lot, you can turn right (south)
and head up the hill to the Jordan Pond House for an Acadia
tradition of afternoon tea and popovers, with a grand view
of the pond and the Bubbles as nature's backdrop.

Miles and Directions

0.0 Jordan Pond Path trailhead. At the end of the boat ramp
road, turn right along the graded gravel path and walk along
the eastern shore of the pond.

0.2 Reach the junction with Jordan Pond Nature Trail and continue straight along the eastern shore of the pond.

0.3 Reach the junction with the Bubble and Jordan Ponds Path
(Pond Trail) and continue straight along the eastern shore of
the pond.

1.1 Reach the junction with Jordan Pond Carry and the South
Bubble Trail and continue straight along the eastern shore of
the pond.

1.6 Reach the junction with Bubbles Divide, which goes northeast through the gap between North and South Bubbles.
Continue along the shore as the path rounds the north side
of the pond.

1.7 Reach the junction with the Deer Brook Trail, which leads up
Penobscot Mountain. Continue along the shore of the pond
as the path now follows the west side.

3.2 Turn left on the carriage road and cross a carriage road
bridge, and turn left again to follow the path as it circles
back to the Jordan Pond north lot.

3.3 Return to the trailhead, completing the loop.

14 Bubbles Divide (Bubble Rock Trail)

A moderate hike with some steep stretches brings you to 360-degree views from South Bubble and an up-close perspective of Bubble Rock, that precariously perched glacial erratic visible from the Park Loop Road. From South Bubble, Jordan Pond and the Atlantic Ocean are to the south, Pemetic Mountain to the east, North Bubble to the north, and Sargent and Penobscot Mountains to the west.

Distance: 1.0 mile out and back

Approximate hiking time: 1 hour

Difficulty: Moderate to more challenging

Trail surface: Forest floor, rock ledges

Best season: Spring through fall, particularly early morning or late afternoon in summer to avoid crowds

Other trail users: Rock climbers accessing the South Bubble cliffs

Canine compatibility: Leashed dogs permitted

Map: USGS Acadia National Park and Vicinity

Special considerations: No facilities at trailhead; chemical toilet at Jordan Pond north lot; full seasonal facilities at Jordan Pond House, a short drive away

Finding the trailhead: From the park's visitor center, drive south on the Park Loop Road for about 6 miles, past the Cadillac Mountain entrance and the Bubble Pond parking lot, to the Bubble Rock parking lot on the right (west) side of the road. The trailhead departs from the Bubble Rock parking lot. The closest Island Explorer stop is Bubble Pond on the Jordan Pond and Loop Road lines, but you'll want to ask if the bus driver can let you off at the Bubble Rock parking lot. **GPS:** N44 34.09' / W068 25.02'

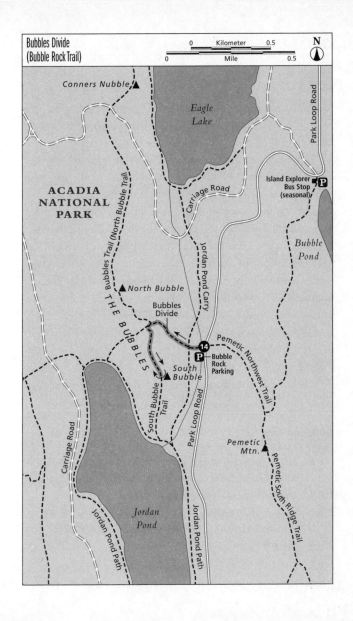

Bubbles Divide
(Bubble Rock Trail)

0   Kilometer   0.5

0   Mile   0.5

N

Conners Nubble ▲

Eagle
Lake

Park Loop Road

ACADIA
NATIONAL
PARK

Carriage Road

Island Explorer
Bus Stop
(seasonal) P

THE BUBBLES Trail (North Bubble Trail)

Jordan Pond Carry

Bubble
Pond

▲ North Bubble

Bubbles
Divide

T H E   B U B B L E S

14

P Bubble
Rock Parking

Pemetic Northwest Trail

South Bubble Trail

▲ South
Bubble

Park Loop Road

Pemetic
Mtn. ▲

Carriage Road

Jordan Pond Path

Jordan
Pond

Jordan Pond Path

Pemetic South Ridge Trail

The Hike

By going up into the gap between South and North Bubbles, this trail provides the shortest ascent to either of the rounded mountains that overlook Jordan Pond. The trip also goes to Bubble Rock, a glacially deposited boulder known as an erratic, which sits atop South Bubble.

Heading west from the Bubble Rock parking lot, the trail crosses Jordan Pond Carry at 0.1 mile. At the junction with the Bubbles Trail (North Bubble Trail) at 0.2 mile, stay straight. At the junction with the South Bubble Trail at 0.3 mile, turn left (south) to South Bubble and Bubble Rock.

Follow the blue blazes and cairns along the trail, and reach the 768-foot South Bubble summit at 0.5 mile. A sign points left to nearby Bubble Rock, dumped here by glaciers countless years ago from a spot more than 20 miles to the northeast, according to the National Park Service.

Return the way you came, although hardy hikers can make a 1.4-mile loop by heading steeply down the South Bubble Trail to the shores of Jordan Pond and turning sharply left (northeast) on Jordan Pond Carry and then right (east) on Bubbles Divide back to the parking lot.

Miles and Directions

0.0 Bubbles Divide trailhead, leaving from the Bubble Rock parking lot on the right (west) side of the Park Loop Road.

0.1 Cross the junction with Jordan Pond Carry.

0.2 Reach the junction with the Bubbles Trail, which comes in from the right (north), but stay straight on Bubbles Divide.

0.3 Turn left (south) onto the South Bubble Trail.

0.5 Reach the South Bubble summit and Bubble Rock.

1.0 Return to the trailhead.

Mount Desert Island
West of Somes Sound

This is the quieter side of the island. The major "best easy" Acadia National Park trails on the west side of Mount Desert Island go up or around such landmarks as Acadia and Flying Mountains, Beech Mountain, Beech Cliff, and Ship Harbor.

The most popular routes in the western mountains of the park are the Acadia and Flying Mountain Trails, which offer close-up views of Somes Sound, the only fjord-like estuary on the East Coast of the United States; the trail up Beech Mountain to its fire tower; and the route to Beech Cliff, with its views down to Echo Lake.

The popular and easy trails to Ship Harbor, Wonderland, and Bass Harbor Head Light are near Bass Harbor. They go along the rocky pink granite shore that makes Acadia stand out.

15 Acadia Mountain Trail

The hike to 681-foot Acadia Mountain is along one of the older trails in the park and leads to a beautiful outlook of Somes Sound, the only fjord on the Atlantic coast of the United States, and toward nearby mountains such as Norumbega and Beech. Another good option is a short side trip to Man o' War Brook, named for the French and British warships in the 1700s that came to get drinkable water where the brook cascades into Somes Sound.

Distance: 2.8-mile lollipop
Approximate hiking time: 1.5 to 2 hours
Difficulty: More challenging
Trail surface: Forest floor, rock ledges
Best season: Spring to fall, particularly early morning or late afternoon in the summer to avoid the crowds
Other trail users: Horseback riders who are allowed on the Man o' War Brook Fire Road section of the hike
Canine compatibility: Leashed dogs permitted but not recommended because of some steep sections
Map: USGS Acadia National Park and Vicinity
Special considerations: Chemical toilet

Finding the trailhead: From Somesville head south on ME 102 for about 3 miles, past Ikes Point, to the Acadia Mountain parking lot on the right (west) side of ME 102. The trailhead is on the left (east) side of the road; be careful crossing the high-speed road. The closest Island Explorer bus stop is at Echo Lake on the Southwest Harbor line, more than a mile south, but you may be able to ask the bus driver to let you off if it is safe to do so. The park service is working on developing a new, more conveniently located bus stop for this popular trail. **GPS:** N44 32.18' / W068 33.25'

The Hike

A popular trek on the west side of Somes Sound because of its great views, the Acadia Mountain Trail also offers a couple of unusual features: It goes along the sole mountain ridge on Mount Desert Island that goes east to west instead of north to south, and it takes you to a waterfall that tumbles into Somes Sound.

Benjamin F. DeCosta, who explored more remote parts of the island for his *Rambles in Mount Desert,* described this trail in 1871, around the time the island first became quite popular with hikers, according to *Pathmakers,* by the National Park Service's Olmsted Center for Landscape Preservation.

Formerly called Robinson Mountain, Acadia is among many peaks in the park that were renamed under George B. Dorr's leadership as first park superintendent in the early 1900s, according to *Pathmakers.*

The trail is easy at the start. You reach a junction with the St. Sauveur Trail at 0.1 mile, where you bear left (north). Follow sky-blue blazes through a canopy of cedar and cross the gravel Man o' War Brook Fire Road at 0.2 mile. Continue on the Acadia Mountain Trail, ascending a steep rock crevice and then passing through a deep forest.

Watch your step on this hike. At one point you need to pull yourself up 20-foot rock crevices. The trail continues its steady rise through cedar and pine, then heads up a rocky section with switchbacks. Good views of the sound are right ahead and you may hear the sounds of boats.

To the west Echo Lake comes into view behind you. The trail levels off a bit, and soon a couple of historic Bates-style cairns tip you off to the peak.

Here, from a rock promontory, you get expansive views of Somes Sound, the village of Somesville to the north, and the Gulf of Maine, Sutton Island, and the rest of the Cranberry Isles to the south. Turn around here for a shorter out-and-back hike of 1.9 miles, or continue on to complete the 2.8-mile loop.

If you choose to go on ahead, a tricky turn on the trail directs you over jagged rock to a second peak of sorts at 1.1 miles. This second broad open summit provides a splendid view—perhaps one of the best on the island.

From here Beech Mountain with its fire tower is to the west; Valley Cove, Flying Mountain, and the Gulf of Maine to the south; and Somes Sound and Norumbega Mountain to the east.

One late spring afternoon on this summit, we saw three turkey vultures soaring over Somes Sound, the birds unmistakable because of their massive size and small red heads.

The trail descends steeply from this second peak, providing close-up views of the sound on the way down. At times it's handy to hold on to trees and rocks while headed down the rock face and crevices.

At 1.7 miles you reach a junction with a spur trail to Man o' War Brook Fire Road and a side trail to Man o' War Brook. Turn left, or east, onto the side trail, and at 1.8 miles, follow stone steps to a nice spot at the base of a waterfall from the brook. When we were there in early June, the waterfall splashed along 20 to 30 feet of rock face and spilled into the sound.

Return to the junction with the spur to the Man o' War Brook Fire Road, and go straight (west) on the spur trail to a major trail intersection with signs pointing to the fire road and other points of interest. Bear right and take the gravel

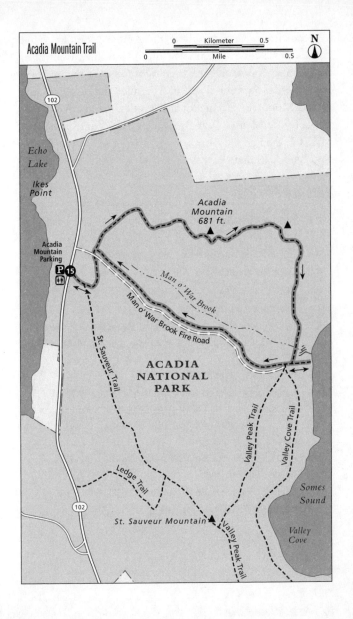

Kilometer
0 0.5

Mile
0 0.5

N

102

Echo
Lake

Ikes
Point

Acadia
Mountain Parking

P 15

Acadia
Mountain
681 ft.

Man o' War Brook

Man o' War Brook Fire Road

ACADIA
NATIONAL
PARK

St. Sauveur Trail

Valley Peak Trail

Valley Cove Trail

Somes
Sound

Ledge Trail

St. Sauveur Mountain

Valley Peak Trail

Valley
Cove

road northwest back to where the Acadia Mountain Trail crosses at 2.6 miles. Turn left (south) into the woods onto the Acadia Mountain Trail, then right (west) at the junction with the St. Sauveur Trail at 2.7 miles, returning to the Acadia Mountain parking lot at 2.8 miles. Alternatively, you can take the Man o' War Brook Fire Road until it ends at ME 102, then go left (south) on ME 102 back to the Acadia Mountain parking lot.

Miles and Directions

0.0 Head out from the Acadia Mountain trailhead on the left (east) side of ME 102.

0.1 At the St. Sauveur Trail junction, bear left (north).

0.2 Cross the gravel Man o' War Brook Fire Road.

0.8 Reach the Acadia Mountain summit.

1.1 Reach a secondary summit.

1.7 At the junction with the spur to Man o' War Brook Fire Road and the spur trail to Man o' War Brook, turn left (east) to the brook.

1.8 Reach Man o' War Brook.

1.9 Return to the junction with the spur trail to Man o' War Brook Fire Road, and head straight (west) to another major trail junction, where you bear right (northwest) to follow the road.

2.6 At the junction with the Acadia Mountain Trail, turn left (south) into the woods.

2.7 Bear right (west) at the St. Sauveur Trail junction.

2.8 Return to ME 102 and the parking lot.

16 Flying Mountain Trail

This hike takes you up one of the lowest peaks in Acadia, yet features one of the best panoramas, overlooking Somes Sound, Fernald Cove, and the Cranberry Isles. There are views of Acadia and Norumbega Mountains and perhaps even of peregrine falcons in flight over nearby Valley Cove.

Distance: 1.2-mile loop
Approximate hiking time: 1 hour
Difficulty: Moderate
Trail surface: Forest floor, rock ledges, gravel road
Best season: Spring through fall, particularly early morning and late afternoon in the summer to avoid the crowds
Other trail users: Boaters and kayakers who let themselves off in Valley Cove for a day hike,

horseback riders who are allowed on the Valley Cove Fire Road section of the hike
Canine compatibility: Leashed dogs permitted but not recommended because of some steep sections
Map: USGS Acadia National Park and Vicinity
Special considerations: No facilities

Finding the trailhead: From Somesville head south on ME 102 for about 4.5 miles, past the St. Sauveur Mountain parking lot. Turn left (east) onto Fernald Point Road and travel about 1 mile to the small parking area at the foot of the gravel Valley Cove Fire Road. The trailhead is on the right (east) side of the parking area. The Island Explorer bus does not stop here. **GPS:** N44 29.93' / W068 31.55'

The Hike

It's easy to see how Flying Mountain gets its name, from the way the trail ascends swiftly to a bird's-eye view. In just 0.3

mile from the parking area, you reach the 284-foot summit and its dramatic vistas.

The trail, first described in the late 1800s, climbs first through deep woods and then up rocky ledges. At one point the ledges serve as stone steps. Once above tree line and at the top of the rock face, you will get views to the southeast of Greening Island and the Cranberry Isles. To the northwest are the rocky cliffs of Valley Peak.

Dominating the view from the summit is the grassy peninsula known as Fernald Point. Across the Narrows at the mouth of Somes Sound is the town of Northeast Harbor, and in the distance are Greening Island and the Cranberry Isles. From here you may look down on kayakers rounding Fernald Point or boaters entering and leaving Somes Sound. You may even hear a ferry blow its whistle in Northeast Harbor, as we did on one of our climbs here.

Some hikers turn around here, content with the views on Flying Mountain. But those who go on will be rewarded with scenes of Somes Sound; Valley Cove; and Norumbega, Acadia, Penobscot, and Sargent Mountains. Some may even be fortunate enough to see or hear peregrine falcons, which have returned to nesting in the cliffs above Valley Cove, one of Acadia's environmental success stories.

Just beyond the summit of Flying Mountain, at 0.4 mile, you will get the first glimpse of the northern reaches of Somes Sound, as well as of Acadia Mountain to the north and Norumbega Mountain on the other side of the sound to the northeast. The ridge of Sargent and Penobscot Mountains is just beyond that of Norumbega.

There's a spur to an overlook to the right (east) before the trail begins its steep descent toward Valley Cove.

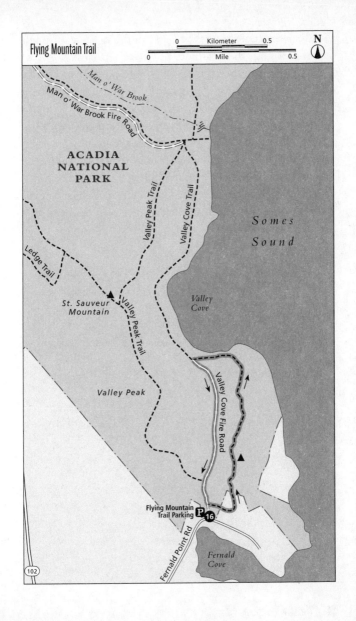

Kilometer

Mile

N

Man o' War Brook

Man o' War Brook Fire Road

ACADIA
NATIONAL
PARK

Valley Peak Trail

Valley Cove Trail

*Somes
Sound*

Ledge Trail

St. Sauveur
Mountain

Valley Peak Trail

*Valley
Cove*

Valley Peak

Valley Cove Fire Road

Flying Mountain
Trail Parking

P 16

Fernald Point Rd

*Fernald
Cove*

102

Once the trail reaches the shore of the cove, it turns left (west) and hugs the coastline, providing up-close views of Valley Cove and the cliffs above it, and possibly of boaters and kayakers who let themselves off along here to take a hike up the back side of Flying Mountain.

At about 0.7 mile you will reach the junction with the gravel Valley Cove Fire Road. Turn left (south) onto the fire road, and loop back in 1.2 miles to the parking area, although hardy hikers can stay straight along the rocky shores of Valley Cove and add on the more challenging 1.0-mile Valley Cove Trail, if it's not closed for peregrine falcon nesting season.

Miles and Directions

0.0 Flying Mountain trailhead, on the east side of the parking area at the foot of the gravel Valley Cove Road.

0.3 Reach the summit of Flying Mountain.

0.7 Turn left at the junction with Valley Cove Fire Road to loop back to the parking area.

1.2 Return to the trailhead.

17 Beech Cliff Loop Trail

Enjoy cliff-top views of Echo Lake and beyond from this easy trail featuring a loop and out-and-back sections. You can see the fire tower on nearby Beech Mountain from a rocky knob. From spring to midsummer peregrine falcons may be nesting in the cliffs below the trail.

Distance: 0.8-mile lollipop
Approximate hiking time: 30 minutes to 1 hour
Difficulty: Easy
Trail surface: Forest floor, graded gravel, rock ledges
Best season: Spring through fall, particularly early morning or late afternoon in the summer to avoid the crowds

Other trail users: Hikers going to the Canada Cliff Trail or coming up a difficult ladder climb from Echo Lake
Canine compatibility: Leashed dogs permitted
Map: USGS Acadia National Park and Vicinity
Special considerations: No facilities

Finding the trailhead: Head south from Somesville on ME 102, and turn right (west) at the flashing yellow light toward Pretty Marsh. Take the second left onto Beech Hill Road, at a sign pointing to Beech Mountain and Beech Cliff. Follow Beech Hill Road south for 3.2 miles to the parking lot at its end. The trailhead leaves from across the parking lot, on the left (east) side of the road. The Island Explorer bus does not stop here, although the Southwest Harbor line lets off at Echo Lake, which is a difficult ladder climb away that is not recommended for the out of shape or faint of heart, and not allowed for dogs. **GPS:** N44 31.53' / W068 34.34'

The Hike

This is the easier of two ways to access Beech Cliff and its views, because the trailhead is basically at the same elevation as the cliff. (The other way is a difficult ladder climb up Beech Cliff from Echo Lake.)

From the parking lot the trail rises gradually through the woods to a junction with the Canada Cliff Trail at 0.2 mile. Bear left (northeast) to the Beech Cliff loop, where you have a choice of taking the inland or the cliff side of the loop. Either way is relatively flat, with some granite steps to make the footing easier, but we prefer getting the views first: Bear right for the cliff side of the loop, reaching Beech Cliff at 0.3 mile.

(If you choose to bear left for the inland side of the loop first, it'll be 0.5 mile from the trailhead before you get to the edge of the cliff.)

From Beech Cliff you can look down on Echo Lake Beach and the Appalachian Mountain Club (AMC) camp—but do not get too close to the edge.

Acadia and St. Sauveur Mountains are farther east. To the south are Somes Sound, the Gulf of Maine, and the Cranberry Isles. And to the southwest is Beech Mountain, with its fire tower. You may also hear the traffic on ME 102, across the lake.

The trail continues along the cliff, then circles inland, closing the loop at 0.6 mile. Bear right (southwest) to return to the parking lot at 0.8 mile.

Miles and Directions

0.0 Beech Cliff Loop trailhead, across the road (east) from the parking lot.

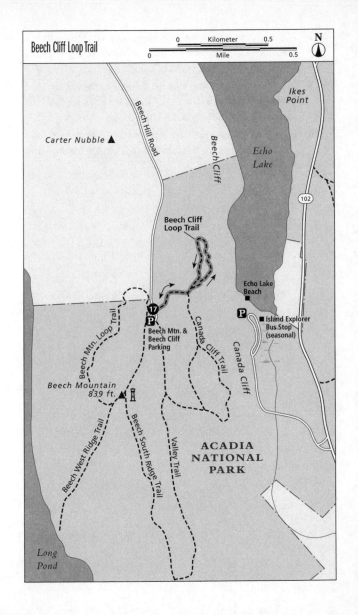

Beech Cliff Loop Trail

0 Kilometer 0.5
0 Mile 0.5

N

Ikes Point

Beech Hill Road

Carter Nubble ▲

Beech Cliff

Echo Lake

Beech Cliff Loop Trail

102

Beech Mtn. Loop Trail

Echo Lake Beach

17 P

Beech Mtn. & Beech Cliff Parking

P ■ Island Explorer Bus Stop (seasonal)

Cliff Trail

Beech Mountain 839 ft. ▲

Canada Cliff

Canada Cliff

Beech West Ridge Trail

Beech South Ridge Trail

Valley Trail

ACADIA NATIONAL PARK

Long Pond

0.2 At the junction with Canada Cliff Trail, bear left (northeast) to the Beech Cliff loop, where you can take the cliff side of the loop first (right) or the inland side (left).

0.3 Reach Beech Cliff, if you take the cliff side of the loop first. Otherwise it'll be 0.5 mile before you reach cliff's edge, if you take the inland side of the loop first.

0.6 Circle back to close the loop at the junction with Canada Cliff Trail, and bear right (southwest) back to the parking lot.

0.8 Return to the trailhead.

18 Beech Mountain Loop Trail

This hike offers great views of Long Pond and Somes Sound, along with a chance to climb to the first platform of the park's only fire tower, a steel structure, still in good condition, atop 839-foot Beech Mountain. The trail is also a good place to watch the migration of hawks; we saw four kestrels dive and soar above us during a hike one fall.

Distance: 1.1-mile loop
Approximate hiking time: 1 hour
Difficulty: Moderate
Trail surface: Forest floor, graded gravel path, rock ledges
Best season: Spring through fall
Other trail users: Hikers coming from the Beech South Ridge or Beech West Ridge Trail, birders
Canine compatibility: Leashed dogs permitted
Map: USGS Acadia National Park and Vicinity
Special considerations: No facilities

Finding the trailhead: Head south from Somesville on ME 102, and turn right (west) at the flashing yellow light toward Pretty Marsh. Take the second left onto Beech Hill Road, at a sign pointing to Beech Mountain and Beech Cliff. Follow Beech Hill Road south for 3.2 miles to the parking lot at its end. The trailhead is at the northwest end of the parking lot. The Island Explorer bus does not stop here, although the Southwest Harbor line lets people off at Echo Lake, a very steep climb away up a ladder trail. **GPS:** N44 31.50' / W068 34.37'

The Hike

Beech Mountain rises from a thin peninsula-like ridge of land sandwiched between Long Pond and Echo Lake, providing views all around. The trail begins off the parking lot and quickly leads to a loop at 0.1 mile.

The western half of this loop was carved in the 1960s as part of "Mission 66," an overhaul effort by the Park Service to celebrate its fiftieth anniversary in 1966. The trail's eastern section is much older, appearing on a 1906 map, according to *Pathmakers,* a report by the Park Service's Olmsted Center for Landscape Preservation.

Bear right (northwest) at the fork to head along the easier Mission 66 way (counterclockwise) around the loop up to the summit. You will soon get spectacular views of Long Pond to the right (west) of the wide-open trail. At 0.6 mile you'll reach the junction with the Beech West Ridge Trail. Bear left (east). A series of log stairs leads to the summit.

At 0.7 mile you'll reach the steel fire tower atop Beech Mountain and the junction with the Beech South Ridge Trail. From the first platform of the fire tower, you can enjoy nearly 360-degree views of the ocean and surrounding mountains. Echo Lake, Acadia Mountain, and St. Sauveur Mountain are to the east, while Southwest Harbor, Northeast Harbor, and the Cranberry Isles are to the southeast and Long Pond is to the west.

According to the Park Service, the fire tower was originally wooden, built around 1937 to 1941 by the Civilian Conservation Corps. It was replaced around 1960 to 1962 with a prefabricated steel tower flown in by helicopter and assembled on-site as part of the Mission 66 move to improve the parks.

The Park Service last staffed the tower in 1976. One or two weekends in October, depending on weather and staffing, the cabin is opened during part of a weekend day.

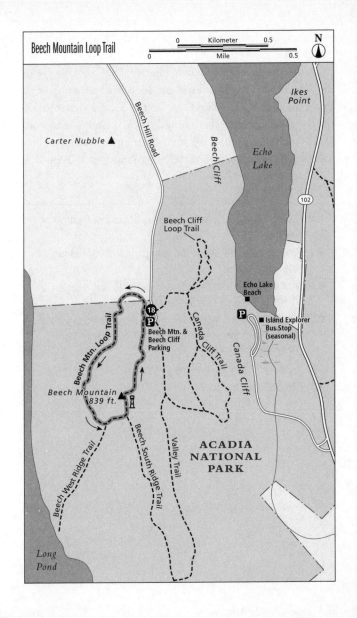

Beech Mountain Loop Trail

Kilometer
0   0.5

Mile
0   0.5

N

Carter Nubble ▲

Beech Hill Road

Beech Cliff

Ikes Point

Echo Lake

102

Beech Cliff Loop Trail

Echo Lake Beach

Island Explorer Bus Stop (seasonal)

Beech Mtn. Loop Trail

18
P
Beech Mtn. & Beech Cliff Parking

Canada Cliff Trail

Beech Mountain 839 ft.

Canada Cliff

Beech West Ridge Trail

Beech South Ridge Trail

Valley Trail

ACADIA NATIONAL PARK

Long Pond

Call the park for current information in October, at (207) 288-3338.

From the summit bear left (north) at the junction with the Beech South Ridge Trail and loop back down quickly along the rough mountain face. Descend along switchbacks, open cliff face, and through boulder fields. Go down a series of stone steps, and then log steps. Bear right (southeast) at a fork at 1.0 mile, and return to the parking area at 1.1 miles.

Miles and Directions

0.0 Beech Mountain Loop Trailhead, at the northwest corner of the parking lot.

0.1 Bear right (northwest) at the fork, going around the loop counterclockwise.

0.6 At the junction with the Beech West Ridge Trail, bear left (east) to circle up Beech Mountain.

0.7 Reach the Beech Mountain summit. Bear left (north) at the junction with the Beech South Ridge Trail to circle back down the mountain.

1.0 Bear right (southeast) at the fork.

1.1 Return to the trailhead.

19 Wonderland

This very easy trail along an old road brings you to pink granite outcrops along the shore and tide pools at low tide. You may see skunk cabbage along the way, and wonder why there are broken-up mussel shells found inland along the trail rather than on the coastline.

Distance: 1.4 miles out and back
Approximate hiking time: 1 hour
Difficulty: Easy
Trail surface: Graded gravel road
Best season: Spring through fall, particularly early morning or late afternoon in the summer to avoid the crowds; low tide for tidal pool exploration

Other trail users: None
Canine compatibility: Leashed dogs permitted
Map: USGS Acadia National Park and Vicinity
Special considerations: Wheelchair accessible with assistance; closest facilities at the Seawall picnic area or Ship Harbor Trail

Finding the trailhead: From Southwest Harbor head south about 1 mile on ME 102. Bear left (southeast) on ME 102A, passing the town of Manset in about 1 mile and Seawall Campground and picnic area in about 3 miles and reaching the Wonderland trailhead in about 4 miles. Parking is on the left (southeast) side of the road. The trail heads southeast along an abandoned gravel road toward the shore. The Island Explorer's Southwest Harbor line stops at Seawall Campground a mile away and passes by Wonderland on the way to Bass Harbor Campground. You may want to ask if the bus driver will let you off at the Wonderland parking area. **GPS:** N44 23.36' / W068 32.01'

The Hike

Once you see the smooth pink granite along the shore, smell the salty sea, and explore the tide pools, you will know why they call this Wonderland.

The very easy trail along an old gravel road starts by winding through dark woods, but a huge, smooth pink-granite rock on the left soon hints at the picture show to come.

At about 0.1 mile go up a slight hill and make your way carefully among some roots and rocks. This is the toughest part of an otherwise very easy, well-graded trail. Skunk cabbage is found along this section of the trail, with its purplish red leaves and yellow flower in early spring and huge green foliage in summer.

Through the trees you begin to see the ocean on the right (southeast). At 0.7 mile the trail brings you to the shore, where the pink granite dramatically meets the sea.

You can spend hours exploring here, especially when low tide exposes tide pools and their diverse marine life, from rockweed to barnacles to green crabs. Be careful of wet rocks, slick seaweed, and sudden waves.

You can also spend countless time exploring inland along the trail, as our nieces Sharon and Michelle did when we hiked this together, wondering about cracked-up seashells and seaweed found far from shore.

We theorized that seagulls must have dropped the mussel shells from midair to open them for food. That was proven later in the trip when we hiked the Bar Island Trail at low tide and witnessed that very seagull feeding activity.

There are many things to wonder about along Wonderland.

Return the way you came.

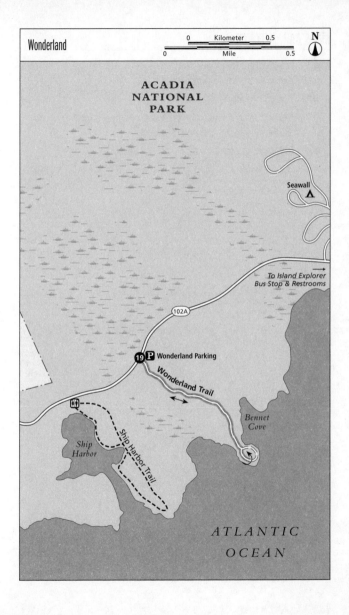

Miles and Directions

0.0 Wonderland trailhead, on the southeast side of ME 102A, at the edge of the parking area.

0.1 The trail heads slightly uphill.

0.7 Reach the shoreline, where you can add on a loop to explore the rocky outcroppings.

1.4 Return to the trailhead.

20 Ship Harbor Trail

This trail features dramatic pink granite cliffs along the shoreline and the opportunity to explore tidal pools and mudflats
at low tide. The hard-packed surface on the first 0.25 mile
of the trail allows easy access to visitors with wheelchairs and
baby strollers, while subsequent sections can provide route-
finding challenges, especially if you take shortcuts across
mudflats, as we discovered one day.

Distance: 1.3-mile figure-eight
loop
Approximate hiking time: 1 hour
Difficulty: Easy
Trail surface: Graded gravel
path, forest floor, rocky shore
Best season: Spring through fall,
particularly early morning or late
afternoon in the summer to avoid
the crowds; low tide to explore
tidal pools
Other trail users: Visitors with

wheelchairs or baby strollers
Canine compatibility: Leashed
dogs permitted
Map: USGS Acadia National Park
and Vicinity
Special considerations: The first
0.25 mile of the trail is hard-
packed surface, making it accessible to visitors with wheelchairs
or baby strollers; chemical toilet
at trailhead

Finding the trailhead: From Southwest Harbor head south about
1 mile on ME 102. Bear left (southeast) on ME 102A, passing the
town of Manset in about 1 mile, Seawall Campground and picnic
area in about 3 miles, and the Wonderland trail parking area in
about 4 miles. The Ship Harbor trailhead is about 0.2 mile beyond
Wonderland. The trailhead parking lot is on the left (south) side of
ME 102A. The Island Explorer's Southwest Harbor line stops at Seawall Campground more than a mile away and passes by Ship Harbor
Trail on the way to Bass Harbor Campground. You may want to ask

if the bus driver will let you off at the Ship Harbor Trail parking area.
GPS: N44 23.17' / W068 32.54'

The Hike

The drama of the sea crashing against the pink granite cliffs of Acadia is the greatest reward of this easy trail. But there are also other, smaller pleasures, like seeing ocean ducks known as common eiders floating at the mouth of Ship Harbor, as we did on one hike, or leisurely exploring the coast at low tide on a late sunny afternoon, as we did on another hike with our nieces Sharon and Michelle.

Though it was once an interpretive trail with a descriptive brochure and signposts providing lessons on glacial action and the local legend that explains the name Ship Harbor, the only reminder of that phase of the trail's history is a wooden sign with a quote from poet Robinson Jeffers, hand-carved under the trail's former name of Ship Harbor Nature Trail: THERE IS WIND IN THE TREE AND THE GRAY OCEAN'S MUSIC ON THE ROCK. With words like these, it's easy to understand why Jeffers inspired Ansel Adams and Edward Abbey.

While there are no longer the fourteen signposts and descriptive brochure, the Ship Harbor Trail is now partly accessible to people with disabilities as a result of modifications in 2002. The first 0.25 mile of the trail is a hard-packed surface that leads to mudflats at low tide, making it accessible to people in wheelchairs or using walking canes and also to parents with young babies in strollers. But the rest of the trail continues to be over rocky, uneven terrain, with some steep stretches.

And there's also the challenge of route finding if you take shortcuts across mudflats, as we discovered one day after our niece Michelle, twelve at the time, wanted to stray from the figure-eight loop trail and had us slosh through the muck. Perhaps if Michelle had known how Ship Harbor got its name—legend has it that during the Revolutionary War, an American ship escaping a British gunboat got stuck in the mud here—she or her older sister Sharon might have had second thoughts. That legend was one of the tidbits in the old nature trail brochure.

Built in 1957 as part of a decade-long Mission 66 program to celebrate the fiftieth anniversary of the National Park Service, according to *Pathmakers,* by the Park Service's Olmsted Center for Landscape Preservation, the trail begins with an open view toward the harbor in the distance and of apple trees from a farm that once stood here.

At the first fork, at 0.1 mile at the base of the figure-eight loop, bear right (south), following the hard-packed surface to the edge of Ship Harbor channel and the mudflats viewable at low tide. The trail now begins to get rocky and uneven as it approaches an intersection at 0.3 mile, in the middle of the figure-eight loop. Bear right to continue along the edge of Ship Harbor channel.

In addition to common eiders that we've seen floating at the mouth of Ship Harbor, it's possible along the trail to catch glimpses of a bald eagle or osprey, or even of such uncommon birds as a palm warbler and an olive-sided flycatcher, according to bird-watching information available at www.nps.gov/acad.

At 0.7 mile, at the mouth of Ship Harbor, you'll reach the rocky shore along the Atlantic, where you can be awed by the dramatic pink cliffs or explore tidal pools at low tide, when barnacles, rockweed, snails, and other sea life are exposed by the receding waters.

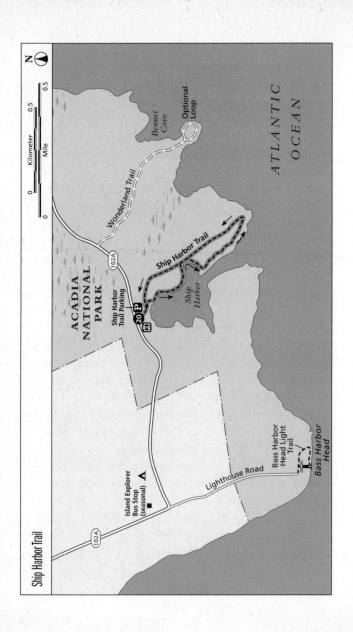

Ship Harbor Trail

Turn left to circle back along the hilly inland section of the figure-eight loop. When you reach an intersection at 1.0 mile back at the center of the figure-eight loop, bear right (northwest) to continue along the hilly inland section of the loop. Or, if you are tempted to return along the easier portion of the loop along the Ship Harbor channel, you can bear left at this intersection instead, to follow the channel northwest back to the trailhead.

At a fork at the base of the figure-eight loop, bear northwest for 0.1 mile to return to the parking lot.

Miles and Directions

0.0   Ship Harbor trailhead, on the left (south) side of ME 102A.

0.1   Bear right (south) at the fork, at the base of the figure-eight loop, and head along the edge of Ship Harbor channel.

0.3   At the intersection in the middle of the figure-eight loop, bear right again to continue along the edge of Ship Harbor channel.

0.7   Reach the rocky shoreline along the Atlantic and turn left (northwest) to circle back along the hilly inland section of the figure-eight loop.

1.0   At the intersection in the middle of the figure-eight loop, bear right (northwest) to continue along the hilly inland section.

1.2   Reach the fork at the base of the figure-eight loop and bear right (northwest) to head back to the parking lot.

1.3   Return to the trailhead.

21 Bass Harbor Head Light Trail

Get a close-up view of the only lighthouse on Mount Desert Island, which continues to guide boaters safely into Bass Harbor with its red beacon. Stairs bring you down the steep bluff to an overlook providing views not only of Bass Harbor Head Light but also of Blue Hill Bay and Swans Island.

Distance: 0.2 mile out and back
Approximate hiking time: 30 minutes
Difficulty: Moderate
Trail surface: Wooden deck and stairs, graded gravel path, rock ledges and steps
Best season: Spring through fall, particularly early morning or late afternoon in the summer to avoid the crowds
Other trail users: None
Canine compatibility: Leashed dogs permitted

Map: USGS Acadia National Park and Vicinity
Special considerations: Chemical toilet. The automated lighthouse is not open to the public, and neither is the former lighthouse keeper's house, which now serves as Coast Guard housing. Hike the trail only in safe conditions; that is, not when it's stormy or when surf is crashing against the cliffs.

Finding the trailhead: From Bass Harbor head south about 0.6 mile on ME 102A until you reach a sharp curve in the road, as ME 102A heads left (east). Go straight ahead (south) on the 0.5-mile dead-end Lighthouse Road that takes you to the Bass Harbor Head Light parking lot. The trail leads from the left (southeastern) edge of the parking lot. The Island Explorer bus does not stop here, although the Southwest Harbor line has a Bass Harbor Campground stop near the beginning of the dead-end road to the lighthouse. **GPS:** N44 22.25' / W068 33.72'

The Hike

Maine is synonymous with not only lobster but also lighthouses.

More than sixty towering beacons still stand guard along the state's 3,500 miles of rocky coastline, with perhaps one of the most photogenic being Bass Harbor Head Light in Acadia National Park. Certainly the contrast of Acadia's distinctive pink granite against the lighthouse's white tower makes for a picture-postcard view, and many visitors come to create a picture of their own.

Built in 1858, the lighthouse even today guides boaters safely in and out of Bass Harbor and Blue Hill Bay with its now-automated red beacon.

The trail begins on the left (southeastern) edge of the parking lot. Head southeast along the trail through the woods, go steeply down the wooden stairs, and loop back along the rocks toward the lighthouse to an overlook.

While the length of the trail, only 0.1 mile one-way to the overlook, makes it seem easy, its steepness, even if it is down wooden stairs, makes it moderately difficult. Take your time. Let the stunning views take your breath away, and not overexertion.

From the overlook the view includes Bass Harbor Head Light, the ocean, and outlying islands, including Swans Island, which has a year-round population serviced by a vehicle ferry from Bass Harbor.

If you clamber along the rocks to get different perspectives, as our nieces did on a trip here, be careful. The rocks can be slippery, especially when wet.

Return the way you came.

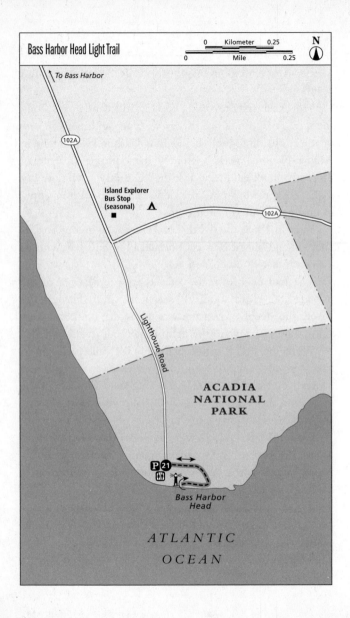

Bass Harbor Head Light Trail

0   Kilometer   0.25
0   Mile   0.25

N

To Bass Harbor

102A

Island Explorer
Bus Stop
(seasonal)

102A

Lighthouse Road

ACADIA
NATIONAL
PARK

P 21

Bass Harbor
Head

ATLANTIC
OCEAN

Miles and Directions

0.0 Bass Harbor Head Light trailhead, on the left (southeastern) edge of the parking lot.

0.1 Reach the overlook at the end of wooden stairs and rock path, with views of Bass Harbor Head Light, Blue Hill Bay, and outlying islands.

0.2 Return to the trailhead.

About the Authors

Dolores Kong and Dan Ring have backpacked all 270 miles of the Appalachian Trail in Maine and have climbed virtually all the peaks that are 4,000 feet and higher in the Northeast. They are members of the White Mountains Four Thousand Footer, the New England Four Thousand Footer, the Adirondack 46Rs, the Northeast 111ers, and the New England Hundred Highest Clubs.

Dolores is a Certified Financial Planner™ professional and Senior Vice President with Winslow, Evans & Crocker, Inc. (Member of FINRA/SIPC), in Boston. A Barnard College graduate, she is also a Pulitzer Prize finalist in public service from her previous career as a staff writer at the *Boston Globe*.

Dan is a writer and has been a Statehouse bureau chief in Boston for a variety of newspapers. He graduated from Boston College with a bachelor's degree in English. Dan and Dolores are married and live outside Boston. They maintain a hiking website, www.fourthousandfooter.com.